Aspects of modern sociology

The social structure of modern Britain

GENERAL EDITORS

John Barron Mays
Eleanor Rathbone Professor of Social Science, University of Liverpool

Maurice Craft
Senior Lecturer in Education, University of Exeter

BY THE SAME AUTHOR

The Sociology of Education (*4th impression 1968*)
Technical Change, the Labour Force and Education (*1967*)
The School as an Organisation (*2nd impression 1969*)
Society and Education in England since 1800 (*2nd impression 1969*)

The Economic Structure

P. W. Musgrave, M.A., Ph.D.

Senior Lecturer in Sociology
University of Aberdeen

Longmans

LONGMANS, GREEN AND CO. LTD
London and Harlow

Associated companies, branches and representatives throughout the world

First published 1969

SBN: 582 48804—4 (*cased*)

582 48805—2 (*paper*)

Set in 11 on 12 point Ehrhardt and
Printed in Great Britain by
Spottiswoode, Ballantyne and Co. Ltd.,
London and Colchester

Contents

Editors' Preface

British higher education is now witnessing a very rapid expansion of teaching and research in the social sciences, and, in particular, in sociology. This new series has been designed for courses offered by universities, colleges of education, colleges of technology, and colleges of further education to meet the needs of students training for social work, teaching and a wide variety of other professions. It does not attempt a comprehensive treatment of the whole field of sociology, but concentrates on the social structure of modern Britain which forms a central feature of most university and college sociology courses in this country. Its purpose is to offer an analysis of our contemporary society through the study of basic demographic, ideological and structural features, and through the study of such major social institutions as the family, education, the economic and political structure, and so on.

The aim has been to produce a series of introductory texts which will in combination form the basis for a sustained course of study, but each volume has been designed as a single whole and can be read in its own right.

We hope that the topics covered in the series will prove attractive to a wide reading public and that, in addition to students, others who wish to know more than is readily available about the nature and structure of their own society will find them of interest.

JOHN BARRON MAYS
MAURICE CRAFT

Foreword

There has been a great increase in the amount of sociological work done recently in Britain. A sizeable proportion of contemporary research and writing is in the field of the sociology of industry. This book uses much of this work, together with the rather greater quantity of available American literature, particularly in Chapters 6 and 7. But the focus in this book is on the economy as a whole, not just on industry, and the approach is no doubt influenced by my upbringing as a Cambridge economist. My hope is that the amalgamation of my former with my adopted discipline will not detract from either, but will rather put both in a fuller perspective, since for me personally sociology has, to adapt a phrase of Professor Homans, brought the men back into economics.

I am very grateful to my colleague, Gordon Horobin, who read this book in draft and made several helpful and constructive criticisms. Naturally final responsibility is mine.

P. W. MUSGRAVE

PART ONE

Economic institutions

Economic ideas I

ECONOMIC SYSTEMS

Characteristics

This is a book about the sociology of economic life. We should be clear from the start what is the focus that such an aim implies. The British economist, Alfred Marshall, defined economics as 'the study of mankind in the ordinary business of life'. This definition is very general, but it does indicate the overall area of interest. Thus, an economist looks at the way in which the scarce resources of, for example, labour and raw materials, that enter into 'business', are allocated between the many goals that a society has. However, we are examining 'the business of life' from the standpoint of a sociologist. The aim will, therefore, be to attempt to uncover the ideas that men hold about the economic institutions that they create and their behaviour within these institutions. In Part I we shall examine economic institutions putting the main stress on Britain, whilst in Part II we shall look at the nature of men's behaviour within these institutions.

A closer definition of 'economic' can be given by following the lead of the German sociologist, Max Weber. He saw the area for study by economics to be those actions by which men satisfy their wants for goods and services; that is, a study of the way certain means are used to satisfy certain ends. The characteristic of economic means is that they are scarce and hence some system must be devised to distribute these resources amongst all the possible goals that the members of any society may have. Choice is always possible. Thus, in a war the decision must be taken whether to have more planes and fewer submarines or vice versa, more airmen and fewer sailors and so on. In this instance the government would decide what its priorities were. In traditional societies the ruling order of priorities that governs most economic choices is determined by custom and is, therefore, unquestioned, so that there is little or no change from generation to generation. In contemporary industrial societies people approach many of their decisions about how to satisfy their needs in a somewhat more rational manner, making assessments of which means to use to attain some particular end. They may buy the cheapest rather than the first article that they see, or they may bargain over its price; in neither case have they taken as given the economic situation that immediately confronts them.

The mention of purchasing introduces a key economic concept, that of exchange. In a traditional economy people usually barter what they already have to gain possession of what they want. They may exchange their surplus of bananas to 'buy' a goat. Such a transaction assumes a double coincidence of wants, namely, that he who has too many bananas and wants a goat must meet one who has a spare goat and needs some bananas. The difficulty may be overcome by arranging a chain of exchanges, but the usual solution nowadays is to use money as a medium of exchange that is acceptable to all. The idea of money has been extended so that it acts not merely as a medium of exchange, but so that it performs several other functions. Thus, money is the unit of account by which we may quote prices to each other, and a store of value so that we can keep our resources through time in a form that will not perish. The ultimate development has been that of credit, whereby exchanges can take place in advance of payment being made, but with a reasonable certainty of eventual full settlement.

Most economic transactions made by barter take place within a very narrow range of acquaintances, but, as modern methods of transport have been developed, the range of economic knowledge has grown and the chances of exchanges have widened. The man in Africa with a surplus of bananas can sell them for money knowing that they will eventually be bought by someone in Britain. There is, in the words of the economist, a market for bananas. Here the word refers not merely to face-to-face dealings in a specific location, a market place, but to the whole of the network of dealings in a commodity. There are still economies in underdeveloped countries that depend mainly on barter and, perhaps, even on local markets, but industrial economies, such as the British, are at the other end of the scale being almost entirely reliant upon markets for all their transactions.

A complex market economy demands certain prerequisites if it is to operate smoothly. It is important that those making economic decisions shall do so with a rational set of mind. Thus, although the order of priorities by which the members of a society determine whether articles are much or little sought after will differ from one society to another, decisions to buy or to make any one article must be made by ranking the alternatives open and choosing that which comes nearest to meeting the end in view. There are degrees of rationality, but the operation of a market economy demands at least an approach to rationality. In addition, social attitudes towards the economy must be favourable, and more particularly, should act to guard, whether by political or legal means, economic property.

Property

Property is another key economic concept. Each social system has its own idea of what is economic property. Almost always some classes of property are excluded from the economic system. In some societies today it is still permissible to own human beings, but not in Britain. Again, in our own society religious bodies have to buy their buildings and pay wages to some of their officials, but they do not sell their 'services' on the market. Furthermore, whatever is considered as economic property may belong to a group or to an individual. The state, a village, or an individual can own a factory. As Kingsley Davis has said, the concept of property answers the question, 'Who exercises what rights in which things?' Today in industrial societies the nature of property is very varied and includes such material things as land, factories, machines, and their products, as well as such immaterial things as the goodwill of a business or knowledge which may be saleable directly or under licence or patent. The idea of property assumes a very large measure of power to hold and enjoy or to dispose.

Though in Britain it is no longer possible to own another man, it is possible to exchange money, a wage, for power over his time and his physical and intellectual capacity. This is an economic fact of very great significance to which frequent reference will be made. The point to be made here is that wages are usually fixed by some form of contract. The concept of property leads logically to that of contract. Through such agreements property rights are made impersonal and formal, and become easily negotiable in a market economy. Often it is not the property itself that can be exchanged, but the actual contract. For example, shares in industrial enterprises are rights in property and it is very often these that are sold rather than the actual factories and machines.

An important category of property in a modern economy is what we call capital, namely, that which enables the production of goods and services. Examples are buildings, tools, stocks of raw materials and finished goods. Such property can be owned by the State, as are the roads and telephone system, or by private citizens. Even in democratic states, however, the state usually has the power of eminent domain, by which it can force a citizen to hand over his property to the state. Thus, in a sense, there is no absolutely private property.

Inequality in the ownership of property has come to be accepted as normal in most societies and this fact indicates some of the important links between the economy and the rest of the social structure—to the political system, which guards public and private property, to the family system, which secures the inheritance of property, and to the system of social stratification, since wealth often gives social status. Certainly in contemporary Britain the ownership of capital leads to power over others and to the possibility of economic inequality where civic equality is said to exist.

CAPITALISM

The laissez-faire system

So far two important economic systems have been mentioned, namely the traditional type of economy based on barter and the *laissez-faire* version of the market economy, which is now to be described in more detail in its capitalistic form. There is a third method of organisation, the planned economy, to which consideration will be given later in this chapter.

Under capitalism most of the productive assets are owned by private individuals and what is produced is largely sold through the market. The capitalist system has developed slowly. At the end of the Middle Ages there was a system that can be called commercial capitalism. The machines needed for production, such as looms for weaving, were at this time not expensive. A system was therefore possible whereby the capitalist owned the stocks of raw materials and the finished goods, but the production was carried out for him on commission by many independent men with small capital who were often part-time farmers. Today the capital required to produce many goods, steel or cars for example, is so great that the characteristic feature of contemporary capitalism is mass-production in factories. This has been called industrial capitalism.

Few own capital; many work for the propertied. Labour is seen as a factor of production that is sold on the market at a price, wages, in the same way that the other factors of production or their products are sold. Economists have traditionally categorised the three other factors as capital, which is exchanged for its price—interest; enterprise, which brings the factors together and earns profits or sustains losses; and land, whose reward is rent. Under a *laissez-faire* system an economic unit incurs costs through buying factors on the market in order to produce goods or services with the goal of making profit. Prices of these factors or their products rise to reflect scarcity and fall to indicate a glut. In answer to these economic signals, factors tend to move to the highest reward and away from the lowest. The sovereign power is in the hands of the consumer. If for some reason he demands more of some product, profits will be made by its suppliers, so that more factors will be drawn into that line of business. Losses will have the opposite effect.

The assumption is that all the actors in this economic drama will be rational and in possession of perfect knowledge in following their self-interest. If, for instance, wage earners did not know that higher wages can be earned in the next town, or knew but preferred to stay where they were, then the *laissez-faire* system would not result in the maximum possible material production. This system works most smoothly where a large number of sellers and buyers are in competition, all eager to undercut one another; where there is a wide knowledge of available products and opportunities so all may take advantage with ease; and where factors and products are homogeneous, so that preferences for particular brands of products are not built up. If such a system were given free play, supply or production would move to meet demand in such a way that self-interest would maximise the national product. Thus was Adam Smith's 'invisible hand' to bring about what Myrdal has called 'the non-purposive achievement of a purpose'. The state did not need to plan because its members planned for it by following their own best interests.

Developments in the laissez-faire system

Though this picture of the system of *laissez-faire* was widely accepted in the nineteenth century, economies did not in practice work in this way. The nearest approximations were probably in the world markets for such agricultural products as wheat or wool. These products were sold by easily describable and homogeneous grades known the world over; after the invention of the electric telegraph their prices were quoted daily throughout the whole network of dealings. However, British economic theorists based their work on the experience of their own country in the world's first industrial revolution, and in many ways their theory gave a powerful explanation of what had happened. These theorists, men like Adam Smith, David Ricardo, and J. S. Mill, came to have a high reputation and their theories to have a normative aspect, in other words to be thought to explain what ought to happen.

This change in emphasis will be found later to have great sociological significance.

But how wrong were these *laissez-faire* explanations? The theory is found in its fullest and also in its most common-sense form in Marshall's great *Principles of Economics*, first published in 1890, and reprinted in eight different editions up to 1920. Marshall firstly assumed on the supply side that there were many producers. But, as the economic size of production grew, a few or even one large producer could often supply the whole demand for a product. Such sole or few producers had monopoly power to fix prices rather than take the price given by the market.

On the demand side consumers were assumed to have perfect knowledge and to be fully rational, but often they were ignorant or paid higher prices than they ought because they were snobs or wished to be conspicuous in their purchases. In addition, like all the classical economists, Marshall assumed that the supply of and the demand for any product were independent of one another. Yet there were monopolies which could control the prices of their products, thereby to a large degree planning what profits they would make. In addition, many firms could also influence the demand for their product by using resources, thereby increasing costs, to advertise, thereby creating irrationality in consumers, who were persuaded to think that this one product was different from that of its competitors though in fact the difference might be negligible or even non-existent. In the 1930s several economists constructed theories of imperfect or monopolistic competition to account for such difficulties. Though these theorists were influential in academic circles they did not have much impact on the public view of the way in which the *laissez-faire* system worked.

Another assumption that was little related to reality was that factors of production moved easily to their highest rewards. Though this may have been true for capital and enterprise, land moved slowly from one use to another, partly because farmers held hard to tradition. However, the assumption of easy mobility was least true of labour who, partly through sheer ignorance or their deep roots in the local community, and partly due to lack of economic resources that would allow them to move themselves and their families elsewhere, remained very slow to move, though some migration of labour did occur.

Perhaps the last assumption is the most astonishing, namely, that there was full employment of resources including labour. Since the mid-eighteenth century when industrial capitalism began there seems to have been a cycle of booms and slumps except in time of wars. It was not until the mid-1930s that the Cambridge economist J. M. (later Lord) Keynes provided a satisfactory explanation of this trade cycle, so that there was the possibility of a policy aimed at ensuring a more permanent state of full employment.

Thus, despite the considerable achievements of Marshall and the other great classical economists, by the mid-1930s notable theoretical inroads had been made into the *laissez-faire* position. But the really powerful criticism came from another and a more political quarter. This critique was more widely known than the theoretical work mentioned above and hence there was the possibility that it would have more effect on economic institutions and behaviour.

THE MARXIST CRITIQUE

There is in Britain a long tradition of criticism of the capitalist system born in the experience of the working class during the early stages of industrialisation. Early in the nineteenth century there was a strong native school of socialists, but the critique that was worked out with most force and was ultimately to have far reaching influence was that of Karl Marx. Taking much of his data from contemporary mid-ninteenth-century accounts of British industrialisation found in government inquiries, Marx outlined his theory that capitalism was but one stage in a historically determined succession of economic systems, each of which had its own mode of social organisation. The ancient economic system relied on a social structure based on slavery; its successor, feudalism, was marked by serfdom; capitalism inevitably had given birth to the wage system.

While Marx readily acknowledged such benefits brought by capitalism as the rapid growth in national wealth, he put his stress on the way in which the capitalist economic system used workers as means to the end of profit. He saw profit as part of the true reward of labour that had been expropriated by the owners of the key type of property, capital, since the workers, having no property, were in the power of those who had, namely the capitalist. It is probably true to say that capitalism bore within itself the seeds of its own critique. The growth in size of economic units led to concentrations of capital which tended to bring extreme inequality of wealth. The tension between rich and poor would suggest criticism of the *laissez-faire* system, although not necessarily of a revolutionary nature. Marx, however, predicted that the labouring poor would grow poor whilst the capitalist grew richer. The result would be a polarisation of the social classes and this would spark off a revolution, leading first to a socialist but ultimately to a communist society.

In the true communist society there would be no scarcity and hence no economic problem of distribution, but until this age of plenty there would be a socialist society, in which the people owned the means of production, thereby ensuring that any profit earned was passed to its rightful owners as part of their wages. The economic system would be based on planning. The quantity and the quality of the goods to be produced and the way in which output was to be distributed amongst all grades of workers would be decided in the light of social goals of an egalitarian nature. Once these overall decisions were made the market would still be cleared in accordance with the principles of supply and demand, but the workings of the day-to-day market would have no effect on future supply, since the planning authority made the decisions that determined this. Nowhere is a purely communist society yet in operation, but planned socialist economies exist in such countries as the U.S.S.R. and Yugoslavia. This planning, linked with the mystical power of Marx's name, has had a powerful influence on the views that many people, particularly in the working class, hold of how an economic system ought to work.

CONTROLLED CAPITALISM

Government planning

Many, both workers and capitalists, acted in their workaday lives as if they believed the *laissez-faire* system to be operating in its ideal form, but political pressure grew, often based on egalitarian principles and sometimes with a Marxist flavour. In the late nineteenth century trade unions were created, partly to press these views in support of the workers and to form a strong base of power. Early in this century the Labour Party was formed to carry this policy to parliament. During the First World War this country experienced large-scale planning for the first time, so that it did not seem out of place to meet the economic difficulties of the interwar years by interfering with the workings of the *laissez-faire* system, already under criticism from the academic economists.

Subsidies were given to agriculture and to certain industries; wide measures of control were extended to the railways and to the coal mining industry. After the Second World War the first majority Labour government took into public ownership several major industries, including coal and the railways. But the intervention that affected the whole economy was the adoption of a full employment policy. Keynes had shown that unused resources of labour and capital could be drawn back into use if the government created money and spent it. Likewise inflation would, at least in theory, be stopped by using taxation to withdraw excess spending power from circulation. By such means the government came to exercise great control over the workings of the *laissez-faire* system; in fact today the state spends about one-fifth of the gross national product.

The scale of planning widens. There are policies for geographical regions, for the coordination of industry as a whole, and for particular industries, such as the power industry. In this latter case, though there were defence considerations, the very high needs of capital, especially in the case of atomic power, have forced the state to step in, where private industry would have had very great difficulty, so as to give birth to a new industry, the atomic industry. Sometimes the government uses the mechanisms of the market to achieve its goals. Thus, it taxes luxuries to stop their consumption and hence to lower production, and subsidises necessaries such as food, thereby raising their output. This type of intervention has the aim of allowing the market to bring about socially acceptable goals.

Business and planning

The values that people hold exert a strong influence on the way they behave. Economic norms regulate behaviour relevant to the economy. Although the increase in the use of planning within the *laissez-faire* system would lead one to expect that what was once the exception is now the rule, there are very large areas of economic behaviour that at least appear unplanned. The result is that many of both propertied and propertyless alike act in their economic affairs as though the assumptions of *laissez-faire* were still true. Particularly important in this respect is the group of the middle and upper middle class who do not necessarily own much property, but are the well-paid managers or professional workers employed by capitalists in commerce or industry, or who are the servants of the growing number of large companies, called joint stock companies, to which reference will be made in the next chapter. In the nineteenth century Marx foretold the polarisation of the classes, but forces were already at work to increase the proportion of salaried managers and other administrative workers in the labour force. Since Marx's day this trend has continued. This group is in a very different social position from the average worker and its members have come to identify themselves more nearly with the capitalist view of the economy than with that of the working class. To a large extent what the Webbs fifty years ago called 'the capitalist domination of the mental environment' remains, though the working class are stronger in their demands for egalitarian intervention than the capitalists, many of whom, however, have for one reason or another come to see great benefits in some planning.

Capitalists, and the managerial groups close to them, have served on government committees regularly since 1914. They have been specially eager to cooperate in planning where their own self-interest has been at stake. An example was over the question of whether Britain should impose a tariff in the interwar period in order to reduce the impact of severe foreign competition. Again, wherever the costs of an enterprise seem greater than the likely profits, help is welcome, and where social considerations also exist the government is willing to intervene. Thus, the costs of a new Atlantic luxury passenger liner or of an integrated sheet steel rolling mill are extremely high, but in the one case national prestige and in the other regional employment policies may be at stake. It is, then, in the interests of both government and businessmen to cooperate, the former providing much of the capital and the latter in return arranging their enterprises to fit the needs of government planning.

In these circumstances there has, not surprisingly, been a rise in Britain and other advanced industrial countries in the degree of planning supported by right wing political parties. The goal has been that the state should keep the workings of the market within bounds of fairness, smooth excessive price movements—often by international cooperation over such commodity prices as those of wheat and rubber, and stimulate or check production in order to preserve a high and stable rate of employment. Planning, as Myrdal has observed, has taken place in an ideological atmosphere of freedom and this development has met many of the political demands of the working class, thereby, perhaps, averting the predicted Marxist revolution.

CONCLUSIONS

With truth J. K. Galbraith has commented, 'We are profoundly conditioned by the theology of the market.' The ideas that those within an economy have of how it works deeply influence the way in which they go about their economic lives. Capitalists and workers in Britain today believe that we have a semiplanned economy that gives each something of what they want. The capitalist has reasonable profits and some security, whilst the worker, though he may fundamentally disagree with capitalism as a system, has a job and on the whole a fair deal. This model of the economic system seems to all to explain most clearly what happens and what ought to happen around them. Such a shared set of assumptions, understandings and values, that is held as an explanation and justification of the strains and complexities of the life around a group, is called by sociologists an ideology. One of the results of such a common feeling is that the system works more smoothly and continues to exist as it is until challenged. And, as has been indicated, the capitalist system contains within itself contradictions that will in all likelihood result in challenge and considerable change. As yet, however, the semiplanned capitalist economic system probably contains a higher content of capitalist than of planning elements in the ideology that governs the behaviour of those at work within it. The next step, therefore, in this analysis must be to examine the way in which this ideology is played out in the market and in forms of property in contemporary Britain, paying particular attention to the influence of both capitalists and the government.

British economic institutions 2

THE CAPITALIST SYSTEM

The market

As a result mainly of market forces there has grown up in Britain a complex network of economic organisations whose main aim is to produce and distribute goods and services. Production takes place in factories and workshops, largely financed by private capital. Semi-finished goods, such as cloth or paper, pass from factory to factory, sometimes being held by warehouses, before they are delivered eventually to the point where they are bought by the final consumer in a shop or through a dealer.

The network of communications supporting the *laissez-faire* market has become extremely complicated and includes, for example, financial institutions that mediate between buyers and sellers. Such institutions as banks supply credit which enables the manufacturer or merchant to hold stocks of raw, semifinished or finished goods until consumers are prepared to buy. There are many specialist financial institutions whose main function is to enable capital to move freely towards the highest reward. Thus the Stock Exchange acts to collect capital and channel it towards enterprises where the highest return may be found. As a result of Britain's early industrialisation London became the centre of world trade in the nineteenth century. This created a demand for specialist financial services so that in London today there still are a large number of bankers and insurance houses that serve world, rather than home, trade.

Such a system of communications helps to articulate the market economy, to ease its operation, so that supply and demand, which never work as smoothly as the theories make it appear, keep more nearly in step. Two particular types of operator in this advanced market economy must be mentioned, namely the speculator and the merchant. Both have incurred some odium at the hands of left-wing critics, mainly because in times of shortage their activities may drive prices further up or down than might otherwise be the case. They do, however, have a positive role in a well-developed market and can be justified in its terms. The speculator justifies his economic existence by buying and selling when in his view the market price is out of line with reality, thereby, if his view is right, making a profit by helping the price in the market to move more easily and without large and sudden changes in the direction in which it must ultimately move because of economic forces. The merchant earns his economic keep by taking risks with his own or with borrowed capital in transporting goods through time rather than through space, since he buys and holds goods until those further down the chain of distribution are ready to take them. Both, therefore, help to smooth the system of communication in the market.

The smooth working of the market economy has resulted in resources, particularly capital and enterprise, moving towards the highest rewards on an international scale. Sometimes international trade is inescapable, since the factor of production, land, is immobile so that it becomes necessary to trade the products of land rather than the factor itself. Thus there are few places where gold or asbestos are found or, again, there are few tracts of land that have the climate to produce rubber or cotton at an economic price. In such cases the raw material or its semifinished products must enter international trade.

Even if Britain had not become the centre of the international trade for such commodities during the nineteenth century, her lack of indigenous raw materials would ultimately have driven her into paying considerable attention to her overseas trade, since she must obtain her supplies of many primary products, and even of food, from overseas. And to do this and retain her high standard of living she must pay for these imports by selling a great deal in foreign markets. In 1965 the United Kingdom exported 24·7 per cent of her gross national product. This trade is carried on against increasingly fierce foreign competition, so that living standards at home depend in a very real sense on our export market.

Market forces also work inside Britain to distribute labour to the positions available within the various industries and occupations in the economy. There has been an increasing tendency for economic tasks to become more specialised in their nature. In a traditional economy a family had to build its own house, grow its own food and make its own clothes. In an advanced economy each of these tasks has been allocated to a number of trades or occupations. This process has in some cases gone very far and, for example, some workers may spend their whole day doing no more than sewing buttons on to men's waistcoats. This division of labour amongst the available work force has brought a very great rise in productivity. There were in 1966 about 26·2 million people in the labour force out of a total population of 54·5 million in the United Kingdom. Of these workers just under 9 million were women. Since one of the important influences on economic behaviour is the type of industrial positions available, the distribution of the work force between industries must be considered. The table below indicates the numbers of those working in the main industrial groupings.

TABLE I

The labour force in 1966

Primary		Secondary		Tertiary	
Agriculture, Fishing	488	Manufacturing industry	9,179	Transport communication	1,651
Mining	635	Construction	1,769	Distributive trades	3,067
		Gas, electricity, water	434	Professional, commercial, services	5,514
				National and local govt.	1,399
	1,123 (4·7%)		11,382 (47·1%)		11,631 (48·2%)

Source. Annual Abstract of Statistics, 1967, pp. 113–16.

Industries have been categorised as primary where they involve agriculture or extractive processes, as secondary if concerned with manufacture, and tertiary when providing services either to consumers or to producers. The proportions in these three categories in 1881 were approximately 13, 50 and 37 per cent in the primary, secondary and tertiary sectors respectively. Comparison of these percentages with those in Table 1 clearly shows the trend towards a larger tertiary sector in the British labour force and this seems to be a tendency that is observable in all industrialising countries.

Property

Very often capitalists have been able to make great profits over a long period because the forces of competition have not worked freely to allow resources to be drawn to these high rewards, thereby bringing the rate of profit to a lower level, more in line with the risk involved. Such imperfections in the market may have been due perhaps to the capitalist owning the sole source of a vital raw material or to his having a monopoly of scarce technical knowledge. As a result of such great inequalities of income, men have been able to build up considerable wealth and to pass it on through time from generation to generation. There has, therefore, come to be a very unequal distribution of wealth. Since wealth gives power over resources to those who own it, this inequality has led to an uneven distribution of power in British society.

Lydall and Tipping found that in 1954 the top 1 per cent of persons of twenty or over owned about 43 per cent of the total net personal capital in Britain. This inequality exerts a major influence in the economy through the ownership of shares in industrial and commercial companies. When a company needs capital for its business, it may sell its shares on the market for capital, namely the Stock Exchange, to those with money to invest. A number of different types of stocks and shares have been evolved to suit the differing degrees of risk that investors are willing to carry. But the ordinary shares in such a joint stock company bear most risk and, hence, gain most reward. The owners of these shares are seen as the owners of the business and have the right to vote on the crucial matter of who shall be the directors of the company or, in other words, to whom they shall delegate the running of the concern. In recent years many companies earning high profits have been able to finance their development without recourse to the Stock Exchange by retaining some of their profits instead of paying them all out to their shareholders as dividends. However, this does not alter the distribution of wealth since the values of the shares of the companies concerned usually rise to take account of their greater resources.

In a study of a representative sample of some 1,700 British joint stock companies of varying size Sargant Florence found that in 1951 the average shareholding was about £500. In the largest fifty-three companies there were approximately 10,000 shareholders, but in many cases there was a considerable concentration of share ownership. Since few shareholders attend company meetings or even bother to vote, a small group that owns even a substantial minority holding is in a position to control the voting and, hence, the policies of the company. This seems to be the case in a large, but declining proportion of British companies. Sargant Florence found that 'in 1936 the average proportion of the total vote held by the largest 20 per cent of shareholders was 30 per cent; by 1951, 19 per cent'.

This decline hides a further change. Because of the increasing flow of money into pension schemes a larger proportion of shares are held by such major institutional investors as insurance companies. Since Sargant Florence concludes that 'two-thirds of the large companies in 1951 were probably not owner controlled', the question then arises, who are the directors who have the control over the economic behaviour of a large part of the labour force? From a number of studies of this problem it seems that about half of the directors are in fact top managers who have a very small holding of capital in their company. Because of this development in the joint stock system some commentators have come to believe that managers often form a self-perpetuating oligarchy, who yearly vote themselves or the successors of their choice into office. Though there may be an element of truth in this position, there have been cases recently in Britain where groups of shareholders have revolted against a board whose actions have been considered detrimental to the long term interests of their company. It would appear that the shareholders, some of whom may still be called great capitalists, even today have the ultimate sanction.

So far in this chapter the emphasis has been on the large enterprise. The criterion of size can be either the capital used or the numbers employed. If one uses the latter measure, the pattern of size is clearly shown in Table 2.

TABLE 2

Size and number of manufacturing establishments in Great Britain, 1961

Number of employees	Number of establishments	%	% of Total employees
11–99	40,049	72·6	20·5
100–499	12,213	22·1	32·2
500–999	1,693	3·1	13·7
1,000 and over	1,206	2·2	33·6
	55,161	100·0	100·0

Source. Annual Abstract of Statistics, 1967, p. 122.

It is quite clear that most people work in units with more than 100 employees, but that the majority of manufacturing units employ less than 100 workers. The real position is understated here, because there is a large, but unknown, number of units with eleven or fewer employees. The number of such establishments in 1961 was probably about 140,000. These enterprises may be run by single entrepreneurs or by partnerships of two or more businessmen. The amount of capital required is on the whole small. There are some industries where costs of entry in the form of machinery and stocks of materials are so low that it is relatively easy to start a new enterprise. Cases in point are the clothing industry, jobbing building and small shops.

For the majority of the labour force the only economic property that they possess is their labour power. To earn a living they must exchange their skill, energy and time on the labour market with a capitalist, or in large factories with a manager working on behalf of a large capitalist or joint stock company. The worker is then supplied with capital equipment with the aid of which production is possible. Normally the conditions of work, including the wage rate and hours, are fixed implicitly or explicitly by a contract. For example, in certain jobs workers are paid time rates, so much per hour worked, whereas in others their wage is calculated on a piece rate, so much per unit of output produced.

Because the employer has the machinery without which the worker is not able to earn his livelihood, and because the worker and his property, namely his labour power, are indivisible, the capitalist has great power over his employees. It is in answer to this situation that labour has organised trade unions to ensure that it has countervailing power against capital. The market for labour has, therefore, become imperfect as employers, and in some industries it is only one or a very few employers, face one or a few unions and by collective bargaining fix the going rates for many workers. This is a very different picture from that of the many sellers and many buyers of the perfect market.

In 1964 there were in Britain 580 registered trade unions with 10·2 million members. Eighteen of these unions had more than 100,000 members. The large unions were of two types, either general unions like the Transport and General Workers' Union, which recruits from a very wide range of industries and trades, or industrial unions like the National Union of Mineworkers, which recruits entirely from one industry. There were also a large number of smaller unions, many of which are craft unions, which look after the interests of one particular type of skilled labour, as for example, the various specialised printing workers' unions.

The unions have inherited from the nineteenth century a legacy of their hard struggle for recognition against the diehard supporters of *laissez-faire*. They have grown to see themselves as not only guarding their members' personal property, namely their labour power, through collective bargaining, but also as fighting for their other rights through political action. Thus the unions have given strong support to socialist policies aimed at ensuring a more egalitarian state. At this point it seems difficult to distinguish the economic from the political role of the worker and of the capitalist. Capital is equated with Conservative and labour with Labour.

THE GOVERNMENT

The market

In the contemporary version of controlled capitalism in Britain the state provides the legal framework within which the capitalists operate largely on market principles. In a rough way the democratic parliamentary system translates the dominant ideology of the time into administrative and legal machinery. What are now considered to be the unfair results of untrammelled *laissez-faire* are checked because the people vote parties into power whose policies are aimed in this direction. The state also steps in to supply goods and services that the market economy does not, but which have come to be considered as socially and economically necessary. In this way free education and health services are provided by the state.

The legal system of a country with a developed market economy expresses the need to guard the rights of property owners as they buy and sell. Laws relate to contracts and the methods of drawing them up. Thus stocks, shares and houses are all subject to legal contracts when exchanged in the market. In addition to setting the rules by which the game will be played the state in Britain has stepped in to reduce market imperfections. For example, in 1965 the Monopolies and Mergers Act was passed to enable the state to control excess monopoly power and to stop those mergers that might create new concentrations of power.

Since 1945 there has been a very low level of unemployment in Britain as a result of adopting a Keynesian full employment policy, but this achievement has been at the cost of a continuous price rise or inflation. Therefore successive governments have taken measures to try to control the way that the market decides prices. In 1947 a wage freeze was proclaimed and lasted about two years; in 1961 there was an unsuccessful demand for a pay pause. In 1965 the Prices and Incomes Board was created. The hope was that it would maintain a continuing dialogue between management, unions and government in order to break the old habit of both demanding and giving inflationary wage rises, and to substitute a more rational basis for equating rises in wages with increases in productivity.

Since the end of the nineteenth century the state has had the power to intervene in the market for labour in order to create statutory wage negotiating machinery where labour is weak. The interests of more than 3·5 million workers are cared for by fifty-seven wage councils under the Act of 1959. The industries concerned are mainly those like agriculture, catering and road haulage, which are difficult to organise in unions because of the scattered nature of the workers concerned. In general, however, the philosophy of the state in interfering in the labour market has matched the ideology of making capitalism fair, since the state has normally only provided a legal framework, as for instance, in ensuring the legal recognition of the unions, and has intervened in negotiations on wages only when asked. The Ministry of Labour has been empowered since 1896 to provide arbitration or conciliation if requested, and mediation if capital and labour fail to agree, especially if the quarrel is at a crucial point in the economy, for example in the docks.

The state has taken other steps to make the market for labour more perfect. Employment exchanges have been established to give workers a more complete knowledge of opportunities and the Youth Employment Service acts in a similar way to enable young people to find jobs as near their wishes as is possible under the prevailing conditions at the time of their entry to the labour market. Measures have been taken to help workers to move from areas of declining industry, and hence of unemployment, to places where jobs are plentiful. Grants are given to cover costs of moving and of living whilst retaining takes place if this is needed. In connection with the latter policy the Industrial Training Act (1964) enacted that Government Training Centres could be established and by 1968 forty-two such centres covering forty trades were retraining about 17,000 persons per year.

So great is the strength of the ideology of free enterprise that there are facilities available for financial aid to be given to small firms to enable them to weather the storms of the free market. The state finances the Industrial and Commercial Finance Corporation, which amongst other responsibilities lends capital to small firms that seem worthwhile investments, but who have not been able to borrow elsewhere. Advice is also available to the 'small man' on the matter of exports from the Board of Trade and in a semi-official form on business matters from the Small Business Centre of the University of Aston.

Much state action in the economy is directed towards maintaining the network of communications that articulate the market, thereby helping to keep its workings nearer to those which full *laissez-faire* would achieve. In this way the Companies Act of 1967 is not only designed to prevent fraud, but also ensures that joint stock companies publish full accounts in such a form that investors can judge more exactly the true returns on capital invested in them. This knowledge should assist capital to move to the highest reward. Special importance in controlling the markets of an economy that is deeply involved in foreign trade must be given to the central bank. In Britain the Bank of England, which was nationalised in 1946 and hence is owned by the state, has the task of policing the monetary system and managing external financial relationships, as well as acting as banker to the government. It therefore plays a crucial role in ensuring a stable monetary climate within which the market economy can operate. Businessmen can have faith in the value of money and in the stability of the foreign exchange rate.

More tangible communications are also provided by the state in a modern economy, though this has not always been the case. Roads were once provided by tolls as is still the case for some trunk roads in the U.S.A. But in contemporary Britain roads are provided by the local and central authorities. The railways, like the roads, are a vital part of the assembly line of the economic system, and are now owned by the state, as are the post and telephone communication services. The provision of weather forecasts for farmers and fishermen also assists in the diffusion of knowledge vital to the proper functioning of the economy. But in all these cases the state has moved beyond the policy of ensuring that the *laissez-faire* system works smoothly to the actual ownership of economic property in that system.

Property

Even in the heyday of *laissez-faire* the state owned some property. There were, for example, government offices and military equipment. But the amount owned was so small that the government was not able to exert much leverage on the economy through its property. However, the state gradually came to take responsibility for ensuring that all economic property, whether privately or publicly owned, is fully used and is not employed in a way that is detrimental to the common interest. Thus, the state lays down minimum standards of health and safety in factories so that those hiring labour, the property of humans that is inseparable from its owners, do not exploit the position of power that they have. The hours of work are controlled, specially in the case of women and children, though very often action taken to guard the interests of this section of the labour force has the effect of controlling the maximum hours that complementary male labour will be able to work.

The state must also guard more intangible social capital, as, for instance, the national stock of knowledge. Thus, educational institutions must be created in order to ensure that there is a sufficient supply of highly trained scientific and technical manpower. In addition the schools may be expected to ensure that the personal qualities of the labour force match the demands of the economy. Leadership is needed so that an environment exists in which economic risks will be taken. Men with capital will feel it safe to lend and those who wish to borrow will feel it worthwhile to do so. Men without capital will think it normal to leave the land and to commit themselves to the industrial labour force.

Not only must each government ensure the 'right' use of capital by whatever criteria are ideologically acceptable at the time, but also capital must today be used to the full. In economics, bygones really are bygones; once a chance of using resources is lost then that chance has been lost for ever. The main way taken to achieve this aim is through a full employment policy. Whereas the overall rate of unemployment in the United Kingdom during the interwar years varied between 10 and 20 per cent of the insured labour force, since 1945 the range has been reduced to between 1 and 3 per cent. There still are some regional inequalities. Rates are higher in Scotland and Northern Ireland, areas of declining industries, than in the Midlands and South-east England, where the expanding industries are mainly located. Though a rate of even 1 per cent of unemployment still means that hundreds of thousands of human beings are in great distress, the reduction of real suffering through this fall in the rate of unemployment since the war is probably the major social triumph of the economy in this century.

The main method by which any government achieves full employment is by manipulating the budget. Taxes are raised to remove spending power from the economy at a time of inflation or over full employment, and lowered to encourage greater expenditure, thereby drawing spare resources of capital or labour back into use. In addition to yearly changes in the various forms of taxation made at the time of the budget it is possible to gain similar results through altering the regulations governing hire purchase. Raising and lowering the size of the initial deposit needed to make such purchases diminishes and increases the attractiveness of this important form of spending; in this way the flow of money into consumption can be controlled. Furthermore, by its monetary policy the Bank of England can raise or lower the rate of interest, that is the price charged to borrow capital. This has the effect of encouraging or discouraging businessmen from investing and, therefore, influences the demand for the factors of production. The main aim of a full employment policy is to ensure that all the savings of an economy are offset by an equal amount of investment. Thus whatever is saved is not wasted.

The ideology that has governed planning in this country, since the first major interventions in the *laissez-faire* system were made during the first decade of this century, has been that of the British Labour party. Briefly the aim has been to engineer social change gradually through a minimum of planning. Initially intervention was on an *ad hoc* basis, but since the early 1960s an attempt has been made to establish national priorities and to work these out at the level of individual industries. In pursuit of this aim the National Economic Development Council has been set up with subsidiary Economic

Development Councils for each of the major industries. On all these bodies representatives of government, management and trade unions serve. The intention is that plans will be agreed, to which all parties will be committed so that action will go forward smoothly within the government's overall yearly budgetary policy.

Another very important way in which the government exercises leverage upon the contemporary economic system is through its ownership of nationalised industries. To many the reason for the state taking over this economic property was political, namely to check the monopoly power over labour of private owners of capital. But an important result of nationalising the mines, the power industry and communications has been that the control of the government over the economy has grown more widespread. The annual investment in these industries is equal to that of the whole of the private sector in 1966–7. These industries generated 11 per cent of gross domestic product and employed 8 per cent of the labour force. The government also purchases in the market large quantities of other goods and services out of the proceeds of taxation; examples are expenditure on armaments, and on the building of roads and schools. The government has, therefore, very great and wide scope for intervening to ensure the full employment of all economic property. Indeed, heavy unemployment today would only be due to bad planning, or to changes in political goals, or to circumstances in the international economy that are outside the control of any one national power.

So far little mention has been made of the factor of production, land. The state also exercises control over those who own land. Acts of Parliament relating to agriculture enable the government to subsidise the output of farms. This encourages the production of some farm products, for example beef-cattle or wheat, rather than others, thereby distributing agricultural land to certain uses to meet the goals of social policy. Urban land use is also controlled by such measures as those that restrict the building of shops to one area of a town and houses of a certain type to another. A similar principle has been used under the Local Employment Acts since 1960 to divert industry by granting special allowances to firms establishing concerns in particular regions, more particularly those with declining industries, such as

South Wales or Northern Ireland. Even enterprise, the keystone of the capitalist system, receives aid under the contemporary version of the system.

Further assistance comes from the grants given to private industry for the purpose of research. In 1961–2 the British government was meeting about half the expenditure of private industry on research and development, which was running at that time at £367 million. This particular form of aid to enterprise enabled sections of the capitalist system to develop in the way in which the government judged essential for the needs of the overall economy. As in so many of the other examples cited in this chapter the control exerted over the modified capitalist system is once again obtained through the leverage of the market, the central mechanism in the capitalist system for allocating economic property.

CONCLUSION

The contemporary British economy can hardly be called a pure version of capitalism since it is characterised by a mixture of freedom and of control, and of private and of state enterprise. Yet the main channel for control is through the market rather than through direct intervention in the allocation of the factors of production or their products. Much capitalist enterprise is today carried on in large scale units which themselves have great power over the prices at which their goods are sold and over the wages paid to their employees. In order to control these concentrations of power and to check other possible abuses in the way in which the *laissez-faire* capitalist system works the state has become a major productive and bureaucratic body within the economic system. In addition, the state intervenes positively in the economy as, for example, when the provision of better communications enables fuller knowledge to articulate the economy more perfectly.

The goals of control are, therefore, twofold. The negative stress is on checking the capitalist system because of its abuses, but, in addition, positive steps are taken so that capitalists, so far as is possible within contemporary social policy, may draw on the advantages inherent in the system. In this way productive efficiency is raised with the hope that the gross national product will be increased as much as possible and be distributed according to the contemporary criteria of fairness. Adam Smith's 'invisible hand' now works within a glove supplied by the state.

Economic change 3

So far change has been mentioned frequently, but no attempt has been made to treat it as a topic on its own. In this chapter we shall examine various aspects of the problem of economic change, though in this important field, possibly more than in any other, the present state of both economic and sociological thinking is very uncertain.

THEORIES

Some economic theories

The classical economic theorists, particularly Adam Smith, were concerned with economic change and saw as its goal the increase of the national income. To them the *laissez-faire* system had generated great growth and could continue to do so. It was not difficult amidst the poverty of the nineteenth century to assume that men had an infinity of wants and that the more goods they had, the more they would want. Such an assumption provides a dynamic to the economy. The views of the classical economists were paralleled and reinforced by those of Darwinian evolutionary theory. Only the efficient producers survive, whilst the inefficient with high costs either go bankrupt or change so as to become competitive. This process would drive entrepreneurs to seek new ways of production and hence technical change would be brought about. Such innovation would be imitated by competitors in order to earn the higher profits seen to result from the new techniques. In this way both the individual and the social benefit are maximised simultaneously. The profits of the efficient units that survive are large and the needs of the market are filled as cheaply as possible. Progress, as measured by a rapid rise in the national product, is ensured.

A great part of the work of Karl Marx was concerned with economic change. Whereas the classical economists subsumed all causes of change under the heading of market forces, Marx suggested that there were contradictions inherent in economic systems that would force those with different interests to become conscious of these conflicts. In such situations men would pursue their own interests and force change upon the economy. There had been a sequence of such economic change. Slave and master in conflict had given way to peasant and feudal lord, then to capitalist and worker. This system in its turn would give way to a socialist economy. Though the Marxist focus on the central part played by the economy in social change has given greater depth to contemporary analysis of economic change, his actual theory has been largely disproved by historical events, since the capitalist system still seems viable in many societies. Marxists have tried to find excuses for this in order to rescue the theory for their own ideological reasons. Lenin thought that capitalism had been saved from revolution by extending its domain over colonial territories, since this policy had enabled the working classes of the imperialist powers to gain a higher standard of living at the expense of the natives in their colonies. More recently the Russian-Hungarian economist, Varga, has put forward the theory that the nature of capitalism has changed, since most colonies now have their freedom and in most capitalist countries the government has a considerable measure of control. It almost seems as if a slow movement towards an economy where managers are more powerful has been accepted by the Marxists as a stage on the way to the socialist system.

After the Keynesian revolution economists realised that, since full employment could now be ensured, resources would now all be much more fully utilised than formerly. Hence a more rapid growth of the national income became possible and also a more rapid rate of technical change. The forces working towards change that were always present in the *laissez-faire* system could now work more strongly all the time. This implied more goods and services and, therefore, the possibility of a higher material standard of life.

In 1939 just before the war the English economist, Harrod, proposed the first of a number of sophisticated theories of economic growth. His work, together with that of, amongst others, Domar, has enabled economists to predict the future growth pattern of the economy. The Harrod–Domar equation predicts the rate of growth possible for an economy by relating growth to the existing technological conditions and to the propensity to save. Given certain facts about the stock of capital and about the willingness of those in the economy to save rather than consume it is now possible to forecast quite accurately the rate of growth that will be achieved as long as these particular assumptions continue to be true.

However, though the theoretical economic problem may have been largely solved, there remains the question of how to initiate the drive towards development in primitive economies and of how to sustain this process in such industrialised economies as the British. Nor has any adequate economic explanation yet been provided of why individuals have a greater or smaller propensity to save or to consume their income. In the rest of this chapter we shall mainly be examining the problem of sustaining change, especially as it concerns Britain. We shall deal with the question of saving in the next chapter when examining the role of the consumer.

A sociological consideration of change

Economic change may occur within the present framework of the labour force causing but little change in the behaviour expected of workers. It may, however, result in the addition of new units of the same nature as already exist, in which case some workers will have to be taught new roles. Finally, new processes may be involved in which case learning of totally new roles is essential. In each of these cases, even in the first, the role structure of the economy is changed. A more complex division of labour involves a more complex structure of roles; the mix of skilled and less skilled positions is altered. In a traditional economic system roles tend to be ascribed to certain members of the community or to certain sexes and tend to be of a diffuse nature, covering several areas of activity. In a modern economy, however, roles are gained by successful achievement, either on the job or in the educational system, and, at least in theory, more or less anyone can occupy positions which are more specific in the behaviour prescribed than is the case in a traditional economy. Many small family businesses even today are somewhat similar to traditional economies: son follows father as general manager-cum-salesman. However, in the large units that are growing more typical of the modern economy this is not the case; the best man is chosen, often from a number of possible applicants, to do a job that is closely defined. The move from a traditional to a more rational basis in the economy implies, therefore, a move from the former to the latter type of role structure.

Certain purely economic factors work to change the positions available in the economy and the behavioural expectations of those who fill them. Sargant Florence has written of the logic of industry, namely of the fact that in advanced economies there seems to be an inherent logic as a result of which certain economic changes occur in a similar manner whatever the other prevailing social and political conditions. Thus, the same industries tend to be carried on in large-scale units or to be heavily localised (e.g. iron and steel or the car manufacturing industry), whilst the same economic activities seem to be undertaken in small or scattered units (e.g. hairdressing or motor repairing). Furthermore, the rapid diffusion of industrial innovation due to excellent communications ensures that similar techniques are common throughout the world economy. Yet different societies do tend to use the same techniques somewhat differently. For example, they deploy a different labour force on similar machinery and because of this the role structures found in rather similar factories differ from country to country. Very often when technical innovation takes place, the whole structure of management needs to be changed and this in its turn can alter the whole of the structure of power in an economic unit; the new process may require a higher proportion of managers or managers with different training and qualities may become more central in operating the factory. Economic or purely technical change can lead to a psychological unfreezing of the situation so that the management reassesses the whole role structure of the enterprise concerned.

The intention is to examine the source and direction of contemporary economic change in order to see how the role structure of the British economy today is influenced and how the focus of power is altering.

SOURCES OF CHANGE

Internal to the economy

The classical economists, using equilibrium analysis, painted a rather static picture of the economy, almost as though no real change could occur. Within this analysis, however, some change was possible through the mechanism of the market. Marshall in a vivid simile likened the firms in a market to trees in a forest. Some were dying, others were growing; at one level, that of the firm, there was change within the sameness that existed at another level, namely, that of the market. The declining firms gave way to the more efficient or to those that adopted more efficient new methods, possibly to meet changes in market conditions.

The adoption of a new invention is referred to as innovation. All inventions are not immediately or even ever adopted, but in any analysis of economic change it is the innovations that are important. An innovation may directly affect only one industry; a change in the steel industry has its immediate effect only on plants producing steel. Some innovations may be taken up in several industries; the introduction of the tractor had an effect in farming and in building. Finally, a few innovations have a direct effect on all industries; any improvement in communications will influence the whole of the market economy and, hence, all industries that participate in it. Innovations, therefore, have a differential power to change the structure of the economy and of the roles within it.

External to the economy

The interconnections between the various parts of any social system are extremely complex. Here three important sources of economic change will be considered; two have their roots in ideological change, namely in political and moral ideologies. But, first, account must be taken of one social institution, the family, changes within which have an immediate effect on the economy. Changing attitudes towards family size influence the size and age structure of the population. A rise in birth rate provides both a larger market for goods and also a bigger demand for goods specifically produced for younger people; the demand for prams, schools and certain sorts of clothing will rise. Ultimately, the size of the labour force will also increase. At the other end of the life cycle a fall in the death rate will increase the demand for housing specially suited to old couples. Thus it is clear that whatever social forces change, ways of living in the family can ultimately have an impact on the economy.

Certain deeper seated alterations in values have great importance for the economy. Changes in political ideologies have already been mentioned. The move towards a more egalitarian distribution of wealth and income has led to the imposition by successive British governments of taxes to influence the working of the market. Death duties are heavier on large estates than on small in an attempt to stop rich men founding dynasties of wealth. Income taxes hit those with high incomes more heavily to raise money in order to finance welfare schemes for the benefit especially of those who earn low incomes.

Different political élites may hold very different sets of values about the economy and, hence, plan for different patterns and rates of growth or change. The nineteenth-century *laissez-faire* élite had no definite plan, with the result that change occurred step by step through the market. However, in colonial territories the British administrators allowed, albeit unwittingly, what were basically dual economies to evolve; one economic system was aimed to earn maximum profit in such world markets as those for rubber or tin, whilst alongside there remained a second and primitive economy, barely touched by the colonial system. Again, the ruling élite in controlled economies, whether akin to the almost completely planned version of the U.S.S.R. or to the welfare state version in Britain, intervene in the economy in very different manners according to their particular political ideologies. The decision to make or plan for war is also a political one with important implications for the economy, since it results in resources of labour and capital being shifted from one industry to another. The rate of growth in certain industries may be speeded up by war or by rearmament. The example of the British electronics industry since 1939 may be cited; war, threat of war and the closely related space race have all played their part in its rise.

Another ideological field that affects the economy is that area of morals, often based on religious belief. One of the best known of all sociological generalisations is relevant here. This is Max Weber's hypothesis about the Protestant Ethic, in which he stated that certain changes in religious views about the time of the Reformation had the effect of changing the way in which the Protestants behaved in their economic actions. Another similar case is that of the recent conversion of many Chinese to Marxism which has had a very distinct effect on their economic behaviour. Ideological revolutions affect most social institutions, but particularly such salient institutions as the economy.

DIRECTION OF CHANGE

Division of labour

One tendency of the contemporary economy is towards an increasingly fine division of labour. The classification of occupations used in the 1961 Census of Britain gave over 35,000 different occupations. These varied from jobs for which much education was needed and that carried great responsibility, such as bank managers, through such skilled craftsmen as watch repairers, to unskilled tasks with little responsibility for which a bare minimum of instruction is necessary as, for instance, a road sweeper. It is quite clear from these cases that there is a close connection between the division of labour in the economy and the social differentiation that exists along class lines in Britain today. The increasing size of unit needed for efficient production has been the main cause of this change in the nature of the labour force. An excellent demonstration of the way in which large scale production can through efficiency lower price is to be found in the early history of the Model T Ford. In 1908–9 10,607 cars were made at a price of $850; by 1916–17, 730,041 were made, but the price had fallen to $360.

Mass production changes the nature of the work to be done in one or both of the following ways; either the task in hand or the parts to be assembled are standardised. Economic roles, therefore, become narrower, more repetitive and less interesting. It is because of this that many workers become alienated from their work, ceasing to be really interested in what they do. This process logically depends upon the type of technology in use rather than in size *per se*. Factories exist where the labour force is small, but yet tasks are finely subdivided and the nature of the work seems soul-destroying to the workers; many small garment-making factories are in this category. Likewise it is possible to imagine a large factory where the majority of workers are craftsmen with much control over their own work; this is the case in much of the British heavy engineering industry where large unique products, such as electric generators for hydroplants, are constructed.

Bureaucratisation

The structure of economic organisations has several dimensions. The division of labour is one. Others are subsumed under the general heading of 'bureaucracy', a term used by sociologists without any emotional overtones to refer to the following closely interrelated phenomena. The positions of power in an organisation may be defined and ordered in a hierarchy with differing authority. The shape of the management structure will be carefully worked out, often on the basis of a 'line' from the general manager through departmental and assistant managers to foremen and workers with a 'staff' of researchers, maintenance men and other specialists to service the line in its task of production. Rules of procedure are drawn up and formalised so that all know how to behave and who has the authority for various categories of decisions. As in the case of the division of labour, bureaucracy is more common in large than in small organisations, but there is no necessary logical connection with size. Empirically economic units where only a few are employed are found organised on a relatively complex bureaucratic basis; examples would be a supermarket or a branch bank.

Business management has moved gradually over the last century to a greater degree of bureaucracy. Thus, foreign competition has often compelled the creation of a sales staff; growth in size has forced the creation of a central planning body to coordinate production in many large companies; the greater reliance on science in industry has driven those in control of firms to overcome their distrust and to appoint scientific research staff. In other words the tertiary sector of the labour force has grown as a proportion of the whole. The extent of this change, even in as short a period as one decade, can be seen in Table 3.

TABLE 3

Distribution of the U.K. labour force by occupational groups (%)

Occupational group	1951	1961
Farmers, working proprietors, etc.	6·7	6·8
Directors, managers, administrative and executive staff	3·3	4·1
Clerical and allied occupations	12·3	14·3
Professional and technical occupations	6·6	9·0
All manual occupations	71·1	65·9
	100·0	100·1

Source. Manpower Studies No. 6, 1967, p. 34.

As the structure of the labour force changes, so recruitment to it must move towards a greater stress on those who have the requisite education, or professional and craft skills that are demanded by a bureaucratic structure. Furthermore, as a result of the coming of full employment the rate of technical change has increased so that knowledge and skills can become obsolete before men are due to retire. A problem that is growing in importance for the contemporary British labour force is that of how to retrain quickly the men and women who find themselves out of work because of the introduction of new techniques about which they are ignorant.

Rationality

The bureaucratisation of the economy is one more sign of the greater degree of rationality to be found throughout modern society. Rationality involves the questioning of goals and the balancing of various means to reach any given goal. Here the rationality is applied to management in that managerial positions now usually go to those who achieve them on some demonstrable criteria of worth rather than to a friend or to a relative, that is on personal grounds. The behaviour expected in managerial positions is now more exactly specified. A clear indication of this is the way in which the methods of scientific management are now much used in industry. Business consultants are experts in changing role structures. Their work can be described in sociological terms as the rearranging of positions in the industrial labour force and of their attendant role expectations in a more efficient manner than the present one or in the most efficient way to meet new technical conditions.

The more rational approach now found in the economy is perhaps seen best in the increasing utilisation of industrial processes that rely heavily on science. Much of this process can be seen in the changing pattern of fuel usage in the United Kingdom. Between 1952 and 1964 the consumption of coal dropped by about 40 per cent, whilst that of electricity rose by 120 per cent and of oil by 217 per cent and that of gas stayed more or less stable, rising by 3 per cent. These statistics are indicators of the huge growth of the petrochemical industry, of the electric and new electronics industries, and of the artificial fibre industry, all heavily dependent upon processes of a complex scientific nature.

One of the symbols of the contemporary reliance of industry on science is 'automation'. This word usually refers to the application to large units of capital of mechanisms for control that depend upon the automatic feedback of information more usually supplied by the man in charge of the machine when he corrects small errors in its operation. Very often the mechanism for control depends on that other symbol of applied science, the computer. It is now possible for a large chemical plant or a mill rolling steel plate to operate continuously for twenty-four hours in the day under the control of automatic machinery. The degree of tolerance to be allowed in the chemical mix or in the thickness of the steel is preset into the control mechanism and any variations are dealt with by the machine itself so that the quality of the product can be guaranteed within the tolerated range. Though the men on the machine tend to be little more than monitors for most of the time, they do have very great responsibility in that they must keep an expensive and complicated unit working. For this task they require a more complete knowledge of the whole process than was needed by any of the workers on the individual tasks that have been amalgamated into one unit.

The exact influence of automation on the role structure of the labour force is still in doubt, but it would seem that the hierarchy of management will change so that there will be fewer operatives and more managers, technicians and craftsmen. As Banks and Scott have shown, the effect of installing a continuous strip mill in one iron and steel plant had this effect. During the period between 1925 and 1953 when this long reorganisation took place the proportion of maintenance and service men in the labour force rose from 9 to 21 per cent, the proportion of staff increased from 7 to 14 per cent and the proportion of technicians within the total staff rose from 15 to 25 per cent. The computers that often control such automatic processes also bring about important changes in the role structure of the labour force at the managerial level; more particularly the locus of decision making and, therefore, of power, tends to shift upwards. The decisions made formerly by lower management and foremen are programmed onto the computer by highly trained and more senior managers so that the computer can make the necessary decisions. There are two important social effects of automation. First, there is the reaction of the workers on the job to this type of technological development; this problem will be considered in the last chapter. Second, there are the implications of such changes for the educational system, to which we now turn.

The need for education

Several times so far, mention has been made of the need for educated manpower in the contemporary economic system. At every level of entry to the labour force the educational threshold has risen in the last fifty or so years. In most factories entrepreneurs and managers can no longer ground their authority on a traditional knowledge of the job, but must use their specialised, and often very narrow, training as the basis for their power. Furthermore, this specialism may change dramatically under the impact of innovation so that retraining is necessary. This process affects both industrialists and professional men; the engineer must undergo a course on a new technique, whilst the accountant learns of recent changes in the law relating to taxation. The operative also needs a sound basic education in order to cope both with many of the technical demands now put upon him and with the greater degree of responsibility that he often must bear.

Quantitative considerations are also important. The great expansion in the universities and higher technical colleges since 1945 has been aimed to meet the educational needs of the higher levels of management. In 1964 the Industrial Training Act was passed to enable steps to be taken to meet the growing demands for skilled craftsmen and operatives, and for the retraining of men whose skills had become obsolete. For these purposes boards have been established that are responsible for specific industries. They can raise money by levies on their respective industries in order to encourage, or themselves to create, facilities for training.

Various attempts have been made since 1945 to forecast the future needs of the economy for skilled manpower, and more especially for scientists and engineers. However, the committees responsible for these estimates have not been very accurate in their forecasts, mainly because of the way in which needs change by the time the increased supply of educated manpower becomes available. It takes several years to adjust the supply of physicists to a projected need, by which time the industry concerned may no longer require physicists because a further new process that needs another type of skill may well have been adopted, or because the product concerned is no longer competitive. Furthermore, in the interim the industry may have altered the structure of its labour force by employing more technicians and skilled men in conjunction with the few scientists that it has. The shortage may have been solved by *laissez-faire* methods so that the planning intended to cure the shortage merely produces a surplus of trained men who may have difficulty in finding employment.

Though many jobs do not need as high a level of education as it is often fashionable to demand today in those who will fill them, yet in general a higher level is needed than was the case a generation ago. But rapid technical change which is the cause of this tendency is also a complicating factor in that to invest too heavily in a specialism may give a man capabilities that are so specific to one position that he is unable to play a new role thrust upon him by innovation. It is for this reason that a policy of general education, even when leading to specialism, will ensure that the labour force can meet more easily the rapid rate of technical change typical of a modern economic system.

ATTITUDES FAVOURABLE TO CHANGE

There are certain basic preconditions that are necessary for almost any economic change in the contemporary world. These are the presence of law and order, particularly inasmuch as the rights of economic property and contracts are safeguarded; a developed and relatively stable monetary system, which has the trust of members of the society; an adequate network of all types of communications; sufficient supplies of food to feed a labour force committed to industry rather than to agriculture; and, finally, the crucial pool of economic, technical and scientific ideas on which to build contemporary techniques and which can also be recombined in new forms to yield innovations. These preconditions are present in Britain today, but change can still be held back because those who are in strategic and powerful positions may be unsympathetic towards innovation. There are a number of fundamental attitudes that can intervene between innovations and resulting structural changes in the economy. Since the movement towards greater rationality is at the root of so much of contemporary economic change, the relevant attitudes are those focusing upon certain aspects of a more rational approach to the economic role of producer. These are the attitudes held by those within the economy to change itself, to industry, to science and to education. Each will be discussed in turn.

Men may have the knowledge needed to bring about change, but may not wish to apply what is known to practical ends. The Greeks knew much science, but showed no desire to apply this knowledge in the economy. Even when individuals are willing to apply what they know, they or those affected may not be willing to take new economic roles quickly. Societies seem to vary in plasticity in this respect. Britain is often criticised for slow reaction to change. It is difficult to substantiate this claim. The type of evidence that may be cited is that British businessmen are slower than those in the U.S.A. in replacing machinery with more up-to-date models. Firms vary in their attitudes towards change. Some are more parochial in approach than others; some are controlled by 'thrusters' and others by 'sleepers'. On the whole, though, there is some evidence to show that those who have high occupational status tend to favour change more than those lower in the labour force; this would seem to be connected with the greater security of employment of those with managerial status than of those workers who are more liable to be directly affected by technological change.

One of the important determinants of whether ideas are applied in the economy is how high a social standing is given to the economy itself. In the Middle Ages the economy was seen as a relatively subordinate social institution, whereas religion was given a much higher status in society. In the nineteenth century in Britain a life spent in politics, the professions or in service in the Empire was seen as of more worth than one spent in industry. Able and well-educated men tended, therefore, to be attracted to careers in sectors other than the economy. Today former pupils of the public schools are moving more easily than was the case in the nineteenth century into industry and commerce, partly because of the diminution of opportunity in more traditional careers, but partly also because of the rise in status of industry as a possible way of earning a living.

The status of science is also crucial. The increasing rationality in approach to many aspects of life that has continued for several centuries now is nowhere seen more clearly than in the move towards a greater use of science in industry. This rational approach extends today beyond the application of pure science in industry to the use of the social sciences through the advice of business consultants and the use of the techniques suggested by modern management theory. But the application of any form of science to the economy must be made by the managers of the firms concerned, and this has been hindered in Britain by the low status that science has had as a school and university subject compared with that given to the arts. Since perhaps the turn of the century a subtle change has occurred in that pure science has become more respectable at the expense of applied science, which has been tainted because of its obvious connection with industry and trade.

The logic of the argument has led to consideration of the attitude towards education. This is very closely related to the attitude towards science, but the members of a modern labour force have not only to be favourable towards scientific subjects, but also towards the whole field of education since the calls made upon the basic literacy and numeracy of the labour force are today very great. For example, the Indian cotton operative is less productive than his Lancastrian counterpart in large part because he cannot, for example, read a work ticket and is thereby unable to find out for himself the quantity and quality of the yarn that he has to spin; unlike a literate workman he must be told this and much else besides. Furthermore, a highly developed educational system can, whether consciously or unconsciously, influence the degree of commitment that the workers have to the economy and even to one type of economic system rather than another. Much is learnt in the schools of an economic, and of a political, nature that in later life ensures that the worker can easily and efficiently take the roles demanded of him by the type of society in which he lives.

CONCLUSION

There is no one theory that explains change. In this chapter we have been looking at some of the economic and sociological approaches to economic change. This analysis has made clear the extremely far-reaching consequences of economic change. Some have argued that because one can speak of the logic of economic processes and can use the same mode of sociological analysis on the economies of countries of very different political complexions, one can also argue for a convergence in the direction of change in all economic systems. Both capitalist and socialist systems, the argument runs, will move towards each other and in time there will only be a version of the semiplanned welfare state.

But, though the technical and administrative machinery of economic systems may be much the same, the ideologies, whether economic, moral or political, that influence the men in control of the systems are very different. The same capital equipment and land is used together with very similar labour at the command of enterprise, either private or state, to bring about economic change. But the priorities given to the various sectors of the economy—guns or butter—and the spirit in which the economy is run—free or state trade unions—vary greatly from one society to another so that convergence seems a remote consequence despite many developments that may seem very similar. This conclusion merely reiterates the emphasis of the whole of the first part of this book. It is the economic ideas that man has that in large measure govern the economic systems and institutions that they create. These same ideas also have a great influence on behaviour within economic institutions, and in the second part it is to this problem that we must turn.

PART TWO

Economic behaviour

The role of the consumer 4

In the ideology of *laissez-faire* the consumer is sovereign. What he decides to buy governs what producers will supply. Failure to meet the demands of consumers as expressed through the market will result in financial losses and, hence, ultimately in bankruptcy. Business is seen as serving the public. In the contemporary version of the capitalist system the consumer has not the absolute power that he once had, if only because of the growth of advertising, but he does retain some choice of how he will spend his income. This chapter examines the influences that bear upon those playing the role of consumer under the conditions ruling in the contemporary British economic system.

INCOME

Size and distribution

The exact definition of an income raises many difficulties. What unit of time should be considered—a month, a year? And should the income unit be the individual or the whole family? For most purposes income may usefully be defined as 'the net accretion of economic power' to a family over a year. This definition of income includes such benefits in kind as the agricultural labourer's cottage and the company director's car and also emphasises that power over resources is central to the idea of income. The average income per head of all social classes in Britain, measured in real, rather than money, terms has risen since 1945. Thus between 1950 and 1968 the annual increase of the gross domestic product has averaged 2·7 per cent. One good measure of this process is the rise in the number of privately owned vehicles currently licensed; between 1953 and 1964 this rose from 3·8 to 10·1 million.

Despite the overall increase in income there is still a proportion of the population living in very real poverty. In 1965, Abel-Smith and Townsend estimated that about 2 million or 3·8 per cent of the population of Britain were living in households with very low incomes. Their definition of 'low' covered an income less than the basic scale of national assistance plus an allowance to cover rent.

The question of whether in recent years there has been any redistribution of the national income between the social classes is a very complex and closely argued one. Over the last half century the working class would seem to have gained more from the growth in the size of the national cake than from the size of the slice going to them. The drop in the level of unemployment has worked in their favour, but the major gain has come from the growing proportion of the labour force at work in the more productive, and hence on the whole the more highly paying, industries as, for example, the electrical engineering industry. This process was particularly rapid in the war of 1939–45.

The growth of the facilities provided by the welfare state, what Titmuss has referred to as 'a labyrinth of benevolence', has also had some influence on the distribution of income between the classes, though, as Titmuss himself has shown, the middle class has managed to secure a disproportionate share of many of the benefits offered, particularly in the fields of education and medicine. In addition, members of the middle class have been adept at finding loopholes in the taxation system so as to avoid many of the taxes levied with the purpose of redistributing income. It is for such reasons that any statistics of the contemporary distribution of incomes are not very trustworthy. However, Table 4 is included merely to give some indication of the degree of inequality. It can be seen that a very large proportion of the national income accrues to a very small proportion of the total number of incomes.

Thus over 22 per cent of incomes after tax had been paid were in the range £275–499, but the recipients, who number just over a fifth of incomes, receive only about 10 per cent of total income after tax,

TABLE 4

Distribution of incomes in U.K., 1964–5

Lower limit of after tax income range	Number of incomes	% of total number of incomes	% of total income before tax	% of total income after tax
£275	4,786	22·6	9·2	10·1
£500	5,195	24·5	16·6	17·5
£750	4,776	22·5	21·5	22·5
£1,000	5,839	27·6	39·4	40·0
£2,000	488	2·3	8·2	6·9
£4,000	79·4	0·4	3·0	2·1
£6,000	24·9	0·1	2·1	1·0
Total	21,188·3	100·0	100·0	100·1

Source. Annual Abstract of Statistics, 1967, p. 287.

whereas the 0·1 per cent of incomes of £6,000 or over received 2·1 per cent of before-tax income, though this was reduced to 1 per cent as a result of taxation.

Saving versus consuming

Given any income one major decision is whether to spend it all or to save a proportion. Those living on incomes that are small in relation to the minimum standard of life expected in the country concerned are virtually unable to save anything. However, as income rises the proportion of household expenditure spent on food falls. This principle, known as Engels's law, indicates that those with higher incomes have the power to spend more in other directions or to save. But in advanced industrial societies consumers of all social classes seem to grow more sophisticated in their tastes as they become wealthier, so that they tend to buy more expensive food of a better quality. The taste of the working class has become more sophisticated over the last generation; butter now replaces margarine, nylon is worn instead of rayon, wallpaper is used in place of distemper.

Consumers tend to make decisions about buying both durable and non-durable goods in relation to their income in earlier periods and to their current perceptions of what they will earn in the future. This latter influence is important and is determined by such considerations as what consumers judge will be the government's plans to control spending. Between 1954 and 1964 the average annual rise in the index of retail prices was 3·1 per cent. If consumers think that inflation will become more rapid they tend to buy now rather than wait till prices have risen. Again, if they fear an increase in purchase taxes or the imposition of hire purchase restrictions they may make immediate purchases. Many persons now have the power to put off or to expedite purchases, because many, even among the working class, now earn an income that commands more than the basic necessities of life and also because many have the knowledge of how to rearrange their consumption through time by using the facilities offered by hire purchase or bank loans. This adds a mercurial element to consumption and means that consumption is no longer a direct function of income. Indeed, the reverse is often the case, as individuals may arrange to earn more in order to make specific purchases either by 'moonlighting'—doing a second job in the evenings—or by encouraging their wives to go out to work.

The rate of saving is the reciprocal of the rate of consuming. Saving is vital in any industrialised or developing economy, as it releases resources of land, labour and capital that can be invested, thereby allowing a future rise in the national income. There is a paradox here. Without the propensity to save, actual investment is impossible, but the propensity to invest governs whether or not investment will actually take place and, hence, the amount of savings that is actually achieved, because it is only when resources released by the propensity to save are actually invested that income is generated from which saving may be achieved. There are very big fluctuations in the propensity to save out of additions to the national income. Thus in 1951–2 out of each extra £100 of national income nothing was saved, whereas in 1964–5 £38 was saved. Fear of inflation is again an influence, since consumers are chary of saving if the value of their savings will fall rapidly.

Income may, therefore, be split into the following four categories:

discretionary spending or consumption that can be put off or not; other spending, e.g., on day-to-day items; discretionary saving and, finally, contractual saving such as hire purchase or mortgage repayments. The last category is often not seen as saving, but rather as spending, as also is such forced saving as that done through taxation or through deductions from pay to cover state or company pension schemes. Traditional economic theory explains the amount saved in the following way. As income rises, consumption also rises, but not by the same proportion with the result that out of any rise in income a proportion will automatically be saved. The American economist, Duesenberry, has disputed this, showing that for the U.S.A. the amount saved depends on the relative position of an individual on the income scale within his own social group. There is a strong tendency within each social class for people 'to keep up with the Joneses'. This has a differential effect on consumption and, hence, on savings, but within social classes. Thus, a member of the working class, who is at the top end of incomes for his own class, will save more than a member of the middle class, who earns a little more than our man from the working class, because the member of the middle class is at the bottom of his range of incomes and is busy trying to keep up to the consumption of those with higher incomes. In this theory the role expectations of the consumer are influenced by the way in which he perceives himself to be located in the social class system. This very sociological explanation does not fit what little evidence there is for the United Kingdom. Lydall has shown that 'the greater the increase in income, the greater the absolute amount, and the proportion, of net income saved'. The propensities to save and to consume would seem, at least with the present distribution of incomes in the United Kingdom, to be influenced mainly by perceptions of government policy and of the chances of inflation together with the knowledge of how to spread purchases through time, an attribute that varies with social class, being more common in the higher classes.

PATTERNS OF CONSUMPTION

Private consumption

As the income of the British worker in real terms rises, so the disparity between his role as a producer and his role as a consumer grows more obvious. Many members of the working class are in jobs in which the chances of promotion are very low, but in which it is possible for them to earn as much as many members of the middle class. Yet to achieve this income they must do work that is not typical of the experience of the middle class. They have to work overtime or on shifts, perhaps at night, or do heavy manual labour. For workers in such positions the job comes to be seen as a means to achieve the role of consumer of a specific level. An example might be a car assembly worker on an automated production line, who is highly paid for boring work, but who values his job because as a result of it he can afford a relatively high standard of life. Some workers, however, still have a more limited horizon of expectations and are, therefore, less concerned to achieve a pattern of high consumption.

Despite the many market surveys run by industrial concerns very little is known in Britain about the way in which the different social classes allocate their incomes along the various lines of possible expenditure. Though members of the working class are now often buying their own houses—in a sample of relatively well-off working class living in Luton in the early 1960s, 57 per cent were found to own or to be buying their own houses—their role as consumer would seem to be constrained by the patterns typical of their social class. An investigation by Hamilton in Germany found that there were substantial differences in the way each class spent what it earned even where the actual income was the same. Hamilton concluded, 'Income enables the various groups of earners to realise markedly different goals.' In a sense, patterns of expenditure of each social class are outward and manifest signs of the different patterns of values that they hold. There is also evidence to show that, at least in the U.S.A., the lower social classes do not exercise the same degree of deliberateness in purchasing durable goods as do the middle class. Despite their low incomes and need for care, their mode of upbringing does not seem to provide them with the critical ability to be fully rational where this would enable them to allocate their expenditure more efficiently. Yet non-deliberate decision making is not necessarily a sign of capricious buying, as the routine purchase of such foodstuffs as milk, needs little deliberation.

Stone studied a sample of middle-class Chicago housewives in the 1950s and as a result of his findings hypothesised that there were four types of consumer. Thirty-three per cent were called 'economic', since they showed a detached manner. They were young, aspired to high status and saw themselves to be at an economic disadvantage; they had few allegiances in the area in which they were living. There were, therefore, few social constraints on their behaving in a rational manner as consumers. Twenty-eight per cent were 'personalising', having close relationships with the local storekeepers. They seemed to be newcomers of low status, seeking some roots in the area. These consumers were willing to exchange somewhat dearer goods for other rewards such as friendliness. Eighteen per cent were called 'ethical' shoppers. These had lived in the district for a long time, were of higher status and felt they 'ought' to shop there despite the cost. Finally, apart from the few who could not be categorised, 17 per cent were 'apathetic', aiming to eliminate effort in their shopping rather than to seek bargains. Very often these were old people. Though these conclusions are based on American data, what seems clear is that the housewife does not make her decisions about budgeting on purely economic grounds. Despite the existence of a supermarket full of bargains the housewife may continue to use the corner shop because she wants the personal contact with the staff that the supermarket largely eliminates or because the branded, classless goods on offer do not meet the demands that her social position constrain her to make.

Corporate expenditure

Many services are provided corporately. Medical care is supplied by the state because consumers, even if wealthy enough, are not trusted to be wise or knowledgeable enough to buy these services. Education is also provided by the state on the grounds that the *laissez-faire* system is unlikely to provide sufficient by social and egalitarian criteria. Consumers often forget or even complain about this expenditure since they pay for it through taxes rather than at the time of consumption. Since in Britain the taxation system is progressive, so that those with higher incomes are taxed at a higher rate than those with lower incomes, the poor should consume these services either free or be heavily subsidised. In fact, as mentioned above, Titmuss has shown that the demand for corporate consumption of welfare services is biased towards the middle class, so that they make a disproportionately heavy use of such services in comparison with the working class.

STYLES OF LIFE

The various patterns of consumption referred to above are governed by certain social considerations. Even such physically based wants as those for food are largely determined by the different eating habits of each social class. However, the demand for food is probably more affected by qualities inherent in the commodity itself than are demands for many other commodities, for instance, for clothes. In cases like the last, the consumer may want to be the same as everyone else ('the bandwagon effect'), to be different from everyone else ('the snob effect') or to be conspicuous ('the Veblen effect').

In other words consumption patterns depend on the style of life that is being claimed. Styles vary and are organised around such attributes as age, sex, or occupation. Teenagers live in one way and doctors in another. If an individual wants to indicate to others the sort of way in which he wishes them to react to him, then he has to make a claim to some mutually recognised position in the social structure. The skills needed to play these roles have to be learnt from specific models. In the nineteenth century role models were supplied by the traditional leisured class or by those who had political, or sometimes economic, power. Today the objects of admiration that set the styles of life are often drawn from an élite that has no political power, namely the élite of the mass media. The clothes and habits of popular stars and of top women models are communicated to the mass audience. Under the commercial stimulus of the leisure industries of clothing and records, and certain parts of the food and drink industry, specific styles of life become fashionable. To play these roles by displaying a certain style is to indicate a claim to a specific status. At a time when high occupational status has come to be seen by many as less open because, for example, of failure to reach grammar school, such claims for status have assumed great importance, and survival amongst one's peers has come to depend upon constant adjustment to the relevant present style of life.

Perhaps the most important determinant of these styles is the stage of the life cycle which a person has reached. Each stage has a different style—the teenager, the young married, the young parent, the grand-parent, the widow or widower. Clearly family size is a key variable, since it will govern the amount of income available for expenditure after buying necessities and allowing for discretionary income. The young unmarried working-class man of twenty-one, already earning his maximum income, can claim a different style of life from that of his workmate who is married with one child and another on the way. In the interwar years there was much talk of the poverty cycle; the arrival of children put many, already on the borderline, into a state of poverty, and their departure from the family, when old enough to marry, allowed their parents to return to a fuller style of life. In the richer Britain of today it is truer, at least for some 80 per cent of the population, to speak of the plenty cycle; the coming of children temporarily removes the chance of living a life of relative plenty, but no longer forces one to occupy the style of life which is stigmatised by many as 'poverty'.

INFLUENCING THE CONSUMER

Consumer literacy

Reisman has spoken of 'consumer literacy', and this form of literacy has to be learnt, as do many similar skills. Some schools teach children the elements of their future role of consumer, but work done in

Edinburgh in the early 1960s by Behrend supports what would be expected, namely that children largely learn about the role of consumer from their parents in much the same way as they do so many of the other roles that they will have to play in later life. Yet 'in Britain quite a number of individuals have only blurred and inaccurate notions of the current price of many commodities'. They are, therefore, in a poor position to compare alternatives and make purchases in the fully rational method posited by the pure version of the *laissez-faire* theory. However, Behrend found that people in similar social circumstances come to develop shared norms of expenditure and a degree of consensus in their judgements of prices. These shared frames of reference have been called 'price images' by Behrend, who suggests that each one is 'an omnibus expression of our style of life and of the income that makes this style possible'.

Though parents are important agents in teaching the role of consumer, particularly in relation to commodities considered to be necessities in the group concerned, contact with others is also crucial. Katz and Lazarsfeld have shown how the personal influence of certain opinion leaders is vital in determining how the majority chose, for example, which films to go to, which magazine to read, or which style of dress to wear. This two-step flow of information affects adults through the mass media as well as through individuals, but for adolescents it seems that the peer group is also important. So powerful may such adolescent learning be that a retroactive process occurs, whereby parents are influenced by what their children have learnt elsewhere and come to purchase different foodstuffs, furnishings or a car thought to be more youthful.

The mass media

The various media thus play an important economic role that is largely unconscious in forming consumers' wants, but they also have an important conscious function as a result of the advertising that they carry. On television, in newspapers and magazines, advertisements work to affect the consumer, since these media are crucial channels through which producers push their influence forward so as to manage the expenditure of those who buy goods and services. Some of this advertising, especially in the trade press, may be termed informational, in that the aim is merely to tell potential consumers of a new product whose purchase may be justified on grounds of health (e.g., a new disinfectant) or of efficiency (e.g., a new fertiliser). Yet much advertising does have the sole aim of making the consumer perceive a specific commodity, service or activity as in some way different from its rival(s) and, hence, as a separate commodity in its own right. In this way consumers come to be attached to one brand of soap or one make of car. Such advertising is often backed by appeals from hero figures, whose authority is based on achievements in other, and often irrelevant, fields. Glossy magazines, both cheap and dear, act as 'taste counsellors', professional advisers on styles of life to purchasers who are uncertain amidst a vast number of alternatives.

CONCLUSION

In a way the consumer still has some sovereignty. There is, first, the decision to save or spend. Next, there is a series of decisions about buying this rather than that commodity, though the choice may be constrained by the dictates of the life style to which he is aspiring. But the consumer can to a great extent be managed. To achieve this goal the producer must take account of the way in which the consumer is rooted in the social structure. The various segments of the role of consumer are all influenced by social considerations. Possibly least effect can be achieved in the case of the basic needs of biological survival, but the rising income per head in Britain has even here allowed more chance of influence to producers; foods and drinks are given images that brand them as belonging to a certain style of life. Most power over consumers can, however, be gained both over the needs of psychological survival, such as the demand for holidays or for leisure activities, and over those demands made to claim status. Producers more and more either create or reinforce the standard packages of temporarily fashionable styles of life that exist in contemporary society and that are associated with various social groups, whether based on class or age or occupation.

Fundamentally neither the consumer nor the producer is sovereign. Marshall saw this to be true in 1890 when he likened the forces of supply and demand at work in the market to the blades of a pair of scissors. Just as both blades were necessary to cut with, so both producer and consumer helped to set the going price. But Marshall's argument was based purely on economic considerations. Ours throws doubt upon the validity today of his assumptions of perfect competition and of the rationality of consumers, but reaches a similar conclusion through a sociological analysis.

The role of the entrepreneur 5

HIS FUNCTION

The economist's view

To the economist enterprise is the fourth factor of production. The consumer is seen as sovereign if the focus is on demand, but the entrepreneur is seen as the moving force on the side of supply. He takes opportunities, often very risky ones, to bring together the other three factors of production, namely land, labour and capital, in the hope of making a profit. Marx saw this as the task of one particular specialist type of labour, the manager. The classical economists, however, laid great stress on two tasks that a manager did not do, since they were of a non-routine nature. These were the taking of risks that bring profit to the successful, but loss to those who fail, and the pioneering of innovation, either from the point of view of the entrepreneur's own firm or from the point of view of the whole economy by, perhaps, introducing a new product. Though great stress has been laid on innovation as such, particularly by the economist Schumpeter, it can be seen as a particular form of risk-taking; the introduction of a new process or product is an economic risk and if successful will be rewarded by profit.

The past

In 1859 Samuel Smiles wrote his book, *Self-Help*, a homily on the qualities of character considered necessary for success in mid-Victorian Britain. This work was immensely popular and sold 20,000 copies in its first year, indicating the powerful hold that the idea of the self-made man had at the time. This image of the entrepreneur was also common in the U.S.A. The equivalent figure was Alger Hiss, whose story purported to show the virtues needed for a country boy to make good in the city, a goal then coming to be seen as worthwhile above all others. In fact, in the U.S.A. this story was something of a myth, as work gathered together by Miller has shown. A sample of men holding key top posts during the 1870s was drawn from the major companies in textiles, iron and steel, and railroads, three of the largest American industries. About 90 per cent were sons of high status parents, 50 per cent were born in medium or large sized towns rather than in rural areas, and 67 per cent left school at sixteen or over. Likewise Erickson has shown that in Britain since the mid-nineteenth century, despite the undoubted presence of 'self-made' men, many enterprises in the iron and steel industry and even in the Nottingham hosiery industry where smaller scale units were the norm, were run by men who were well born. In Erickson's sample it was not till those in office in the period 1935–47 were considered that the proportion of those recruited from the lower social classes rose as high as 9 per cent in steel; the same proportion had been reached in hosiery for those holding office in the earlier period of 1905–25. Though the leaders of the steel industry were drawn from families of higher status than those in the hosiery industry, the rate of recruitment of sons or other near relations to family businesses was higher in the steel industry throughout the whole period, though the fall-off in such self-recruitment in the twentieth century has been less in the hosiery industry.

Today

Already the tenor of the analysis has changed and the discussion has come to focus on those in high office in industrial concerns rather than on the traditional single entrepreneur. Yet, before examining the place of enterprise in large corporations it is well to remember that, as has already been indicated, a great number of small concerns still exist in the economy, usually run by a single entrepreneur of the type described by the classical economists. Mayer has shown that in the

U.S.A. the number of economic units has increased at the same rate as the increase in the population. Business enterprise seems a hardy institution despite the high infant mortality rate amongst small enterprises. Such concerns—and failures—are very common in the retail and the service trades where a relatively small amount of capital is needed to start a business.

The threshold of capital in many sectors of the economy is much higher than was the case in the nineteenth century, the supposed heyday of the selfmade man. Large concerns under contemporary conditions are usually run by a board of directors. Sargant Florence found in 1951 that in those large companies with a capital of over £3 million the boards on average had nine members; smaller companies had fewer members. In the larger companies four out of the top eight managers were members of the board and of the largest twenty shareholders 1·5 were on the board. These men act as entrepreneurial teams, exercising corporate enterprise. They display the most important ideological qualities of the traditional entrepreneur, who saw himself as the sole leader and authority in the organisation that he had founded, usually not tolerating any who claimed even near equal power. Members of entrepreneurial teams see themselves as sharing a similar position to the traditional entrepreneur and may either corporately or individually exercise similar qualities of charismatic leadership, based on the dynamic qualities of their personality.

The entrepreneurial team contains a number of key makers of decisions and is supported by a large number of specialists whom Galbraith has christened 'the technostructure'. The role of these managers will be considered in the next chapter. The entrepreneurs have a number of activities which they alone can undertake. Firstly, they take decisions on the raising and the allocation of capital needed in the business. Thus, they may decide to pay for further expansion out of retained profits rather than raise new capital on the Stock Exchange. Secondly, they, acting as the trustees of the shareholders, review and control the operation of the concern, both internally and in its relations with other concerns; very often this role is performed by one member of the team sitting on the board of a company whose activities interlock with his own company. Thirdly, the team decide on the general policy of their company and give instructions to the managers whom they appoint to carry out their policy. Their power and ability to make crucial decisions is largely based on their occupying a central position in the organisation and thereby having sole control of much information that is vital for deciding about ends and means in the company.

In certain circumstances today the state may act as the entrepreneur so as to initiate economic change. This may be because the requirements of capital are too high for a company in the private sector to raise even through the Stock Exchange. It was partly for this reason that prior to nationalisation the steel industry was given aid to set up two continuous strip rolling mills. Another possibility is that special social factors may be considered important, as when the state helped the Cunard company to finance the building of the Q.4 on grounds of national prestige, so that a large British luxury liner should still sail the seven seas. In these cases the entrepreneur is not taking all the risks; the potential losses have been borne by society. The ultimate development is seen in the case of the nationalised industries where the state bears all the risks and, therefore, reaps any profits or stands any losses. Because of the special nature of most of the industries that have been nationalised in Britain there have been many losses to carry and few profits to take.

Even where the state does not intervene the very fact that today many enterprises are so much bigger tends to lower the risks involved, if only on statistical grounds. For example, merely on actuarial grounds the larger an insurance company the more firmly can it predict thefts, accidents and deaths at a specific age; as a result the more easily can it plan a profitable business. Large enterprises can also plan innovation, for instance, by setting a research team a task. Meanwhile the company will go about creating a market for the product envisaged by a phased policy of advertising. A very good example of this latter process is the development and marketing of a new model of a car.

But in the long run in the private sector profits are crucial. Even the best planned innovation may not sell as predicted. One product, perhaps a new artificial fibre, may not fully meet technical requirements, whilst another, for example, a new model of a popular car, may not catch the public fancy as anticipated. There are powerful constraints on the entrepreneurial team to make as large a profit as possible, if not in each year, then certainly over a relatively small number of years. There may be groups of alert shareholders or of institutional investors, for example, insurance companies investing the proceeds of pension schemes, who are keen to watch their own interests by ensuring the maximum possible return on their investment in the company. Or there may be the danger of a more enterprising company taking them over in the belief that they can make a higher return for those who own shares in the company than the present entrepreneurial team is doing. It should be noted that even the nationalised industries are supposed by statute to make a profit 'taking one year with another', though the sanctions upon them are political rather than economic. Modern management techniques are in this respect an aid to enterprise in that in the form of cost accounting the profit motive can be built into the structure of the organisation more firmly than was the case.

Entrepreneurs, therefore, whether working on their own in the traditional way or, as is growing more common, in teams, take decisions on the goals of their companies, deriving their power to do this mainly from their central position in the structure of their organisations, but also sometimes from a charismatic personality. The ideology of the entrepreneur has as its aim the attempt to put a favourable light on the use of this authority. Schumpeter wrote of the 'designing, directing, leading, coordinating function' of the entrepreneur. From a sociological viewpoint the entrepreneur is important for two main reasons. Firstly, he initiates expansion and growth, thereby causing change. Secondly, he occupies a position of authority in the economic system which spills over into such other institutional spheres as politics, both because of the centrality of the economy in society and because of his power over important social resources. Strictly he plays a role in the economic system, and it is from this perspective that the present analysis will proceed. Certain behaviour is expected of the entrepreneur; very briefly, to make profits after a rational consideration of the alternatives by risking his own, or more often today his company's, resources.

ENTREPRENEURIAL BEHAVIOUR

Licensed deviance

The alternatives open to the entrepreneur are largely determined by the values of the society in which he works. Basically he is permitted to deviate by changing the goods and services that he produces within the limits prescribed by his culture. Thus he may put a more efficient motor car or suspender belt on the market, but may not pioneer more efficient non-medical drugs or topless evening dresses. He is a licensed deviant. The role of the entrepreneur permits some changing of norms and the successful entrepreneur builds up a credit of idiosyncrasy on which he may draw. This is based on the value of his past contributions to the economy so that a well-known entrepreneur can in all probability go further beyond the range of conduct permitted by his society than can one who is unknown. This principle is seen clearly at work in the fashion industry where outré clothes are accepted internationally if backed by a well-known French name.

In the U.S.A., and to a somewhat lesser extent in Britian, success is measured largely by such very general criteria as the achievement of an occupation of high status or by the earning of a high income. Thus the goals that are built into the position of entrepreneur well match the standards of society at large. The wealth of the entrepreneur is presumed to show his economic importance and competence. Yet success can also make his role more visible, as in fact is the case with many deviant roles. It is for this reason that in the past the role has often been filled by groups on the margins of society; the Jews in Britain and the Indians in East Africa have historically acted as successful entrepreneurs, who were barely tolerated as full members of the society in whose economic system they played a crucial role. Sometimes success itself has resulted in the successful being rated as marginal; in the nineteenth century many successful British entrepreneurs found great difficulty in being accepted socially by those already given the status which they were claiming because of their wealth.

Economists tend to believe that given the opportunity the entrepreneur will emerge, whereas the position taken here is that it is only when society is structured in the requisite way that this will occur. Opportunities may be present but not taken because it may be that the reward of the capitalist system, namely money, is not rated high in that society. Furthermore, entrepreneurs can create economic opportunities; the man who invented the ball-point pen forced a new writing tool on the world. The important question to be asked is whence in the social structure are those who make or take economic opportunities recruited? But before attempting to answer this question it is first necessary to consider how much deviance is allowed as the base from which change becomes possible. What is the nature of the sanctions against deviance?

Sanctions

All role-playing is controlled by sanctions, that is by rewards for compliance with expected behaviour and punishments for deviance. The behaviour of the entrepreneur is conditioned in this way, though the range and type of innovation permitted may vary through time and by society and even by field of activity. What is condoned in the case of a rag-and-bone man may be condemned in the case of a merchant. The entrepreneur must at least appear to achieve success through 'clean business', though the very existence of the saying 'business is business' implies that practices of dubious morality are recognised as being not uncommon. Some actions that would be theoretically effective in realising larger profits such as cheating the ignorant by diluting milk or providing guests at a banquet with a wine of low quality in place of a better one are morally condemned or even, as in the first case, declared illegal. Existing social relationships may also constrain an entrepreneur; the shopkeepers of small towns act in a neighbourly fashion towards each other rather than actively undercutting their rivals, thus not pressing towards a maximum profit because of feared reprisals of a social, as much as an economic, nature.

There is a considerable body of qualitative evidence to support the view that in the U.S.A. entrepreneurs are expected to show a more open, go-getting, professional approach, whereas in Britain a more restrained, amateur, rule-of-thumb style is approved. In the U.S.A. the main reward for success from such methods is high income, but in Britain many put priority on rewards of status; a knighthood is for many a higher prize than big profits. Successful British entrepreneurs have the problem of converting their monetary success in the economy, an institutional sphere that still carries somewhat low status, into success in other spheres where different criteria rule. Thus, businessmen try to buy themselves into politics by large donations to political parties or to gain power of a very different type by becoming patrons of the arts.

To an economist the main sanctions influencing the entrepreneur are monetary, those of profit and loss. Profit has been shown to have a different meaning in the U.S.A. and in Britain. So too has loss, or more particularly its ultimate form, bankruptcy. In the U.S.A. this is shrugged off as a possible misfortune if things go wrong, but in Britain to be declared a bankrupt carries overtones of moral condemnation, fears of which may inhibit entrepreneurs from taking high risks. Thus factors of a non-economic nature have a strong influence on the way that the sanctions implicit in the *laissez-faire* system work in different social settings.

SOCIALISATION

The sociologist gives the name of socialisation to the process whereby anyone playing a role is moulded by the sanctions at work on him as he fills this position so that he comes to behave as expected, often without conscious thought or a sense of constraint. There are two possibilities. On the one hand a position may attract a certain type of person to it or, on the other hand, those who fill the position may be moulded by playing the role. There is a long tradition of sociological thought and some evidence to support the view that the role of entrepreneur attracts a man with a certain type of personality, though none would deny that, since the process of socialisation is lifelong, entrepreneurs once in a position do change as they play this role. We must now examine the source of recruitment of entrepreneurs by considering various explanations of the way in which the entrepreneurial personality is created.

The Protestant ethic

The classic explanation of the source of the spirit of capitalism was Weber's analysis of the effect of the Reformation on the economic behaviour of Protestants, and particularly of Calvinists. In his series of essays written in 1904–5, *The Protestant Ethic and the Spirit of Capitalism*, Weber stated the thesis that changes in religious ideology indirectly affected behaviour in the economic sphere in that work and saving became more important. Calvinists believe in the doctrine of predestination, namely that God had chosen at birth those who would be saved and those who were to be damned. A hint of the future after death was to be seen in the way in which a man lived his life here on earth. Therefore, the use of wealth for production and the saving of much of the profit yielded by it, rather than its expenditure on splendour as was the Catholic custom, was interpreted as a sign of grace. Work came to be seen as a form of prayer. So to many Protestants the struggle for material improvement and the practice of thrift, behaviour extremely apt for capitalism, became respectable.

Certainly, Holland, a largely Protestant country, led the revolution that ushered in commercial capitalism and Britain pioneered the industrial revolution. Hagen, amongst many others, has shown that even within Protestant Britain there was a disproportionate number of nonconformists amongst the entrepreneurs of the early industrial revolution. There have been criticisms of the Weberian thesis, both because of doubt over the data brought to back it and because it now provides no adequate explanation of the more rapid growth rates of Catholic and non-Christian, when compared with Protestant, countries. There is also evidence of a social psychological nature on leadership which indicates that different types of leader are required in different types of situation. It would, therefore, be odd to expect successful entrepreneurs in large companies to show the same characteristics of personality as those in small enterprises, or even for entrepreneurs in differing lines of business to have the same personal qualities.

Need for achievement

A major theoretical advance has recently been made by McClelland and his associates, who have proposed that during their early socialisation in the family children learn a 'need for achievement'. This is defined as 'a desire to do well, not so much for the sake of social recognition or prestige, but to attain an inner feeling of accomplishment'. The child continually compares his achievement along various dimensions with that of others whom he sees as significant. McClelland has been able to isolate empirically this need for achievement and relate its presence in various ways to economic development. Thus, an analysis of the content of children's literature has shown that twenty-five to fifty years after the introduction of stories containing a strong element of striving and ambition there has been in a number of countries a more rapid rate of economic growth measured by the rate of increase in the national income or in the production of electricity. Other research workers have shown that an upbringing in which parents are supportive and encouraging, and constantly put situations in front of their children that are slightly more difficult than those just overcome, results in a higher need for achievement than do other types of experience. A point worth adding here is that many studies show that the type of upbringing in which children learn a high need for achievement is more commonly found in middle-class than in working-class families.

McClelland has taken Weber's thesis which may be expressed in simple terms as: the ideology of Protestantism → economic development and introduced an intervening variable so that the chain of explanation now runs: Protestantism → independence training in childhood that teaches the child the need for achievement → economic development. This ingenious work does not yet explain why those with a high need for achievement opt to play the role of entrepreneur in the economy. Why do they not become artistic or religious innovators? The causal chain must be related to the social structure; attention must be given to the route by which those with a high need for achievement find their way into the economy.

Before considering this final question of recruitment one other point about socialisation should be made. As the nature of the economic system changes, so may the characteristics of personality that are desirable for those operating the system. More particularly the trend towards a higher proportion of the labour force in the tertiary sector means that the demand has risen for those who can fill bureaucratic positions, and these may well require a different type of personality. Miller and Swanson have shown that in the 1950s in the U.S.A. there seemed to be a change in the way in which families in different parts of the labour force brought up their children. Entrepreneurial families, carefully defined to include only those where the father worked in an enterprise akin to the typical nineteenth-century small concern, prepared their children, often unconsciously, to be go-getters and, hence, to fit similar positions to those of their fathers; bureaucratic families, again carefully defined to cover concerns with a well-developed hierarchy, taught their children to be more cooperative, a characteristic of personality that suited well the type of corporation in which their fathers were employed. In a rather similar way the requirements of personality in those who play the role of entrepreneur may change through time.

RECRUITMENT TO THE ROLE OF ENTREPRENEUR

The roles that are granted high status vary in different societies. In ancient Rome the well-rounded man was given high status, whereas in most contemporary industrial societies it is the specialist who is given most respect. In nineteenth-century Britain, as in imperial Rome, politicians, colonial administrators and soldiers were seen as important; men like Julius Caesar or the Duke of Wellington combined the three roles. Middle-class citizens who aspired to high achievement saw such positions as those at which to aim, and the upper class saw themselves as responsible for the polity, not the economy. At the same period of time in the newly created German Empire Bismarck had made it clear to the middle class that politics was to be the preserve of the upper class and was not, therefore, an avenue to success available to other social classes, but the pathway through the economy was open to them. Thus, ambition for high status, learnt young, plays itself out through different channels for each social class in different societies.

In contemporary Britain norms decree that few women are recruited to the role of entrepreneur. This is partly due to sheer prejudice, since in societies such as the U.S.S.R. where the role of woman is defined in a different way, women carry out many activities which are here deemed as impossible or unsuitable. But there are also genuine grounds for the belief that women find difficulty in filling the role of entrepreneur, since the career of many women is broken by a period of child-bearing and motherhood, during which it is often impossible to undertake a full-time economic role. This means that women cannot keep in touch with the social and technical aspects of business and are unable to function as efficiently as their male competitors.

As has been indicated, even in the nineteenth century many entrepreneurs were middle class by birth. With the gradual rise in the formal education required to run most enterprises the chances that selfmade men might emerge from the working class fell, if only because working-class families were unable to bear the expense of giving their sons the necessary education. Since the start of this century the availability of scholarships to secondary schools has grown and there is more chance of children from working-class homes becoming entrepreneurs or members of entrepreneurial teams. Yet, though the chances are there, many surveys have shown that mainly because of the different way each social class is brought up before ever reaching school it is the middle class that gains most from these wider opportunities. Surveys of upper management by Clements and the Acton Society Trust show that there are still many 'Crown Princes', especially in the line of succession to high positions in the medium-sized companies that are common in such traditional industries as the woollen and cotton textile industries. These sons of their fathers are usually highly educated, often to university level, and are, therefore, well equipped to use the favourable opportunity given to them as a result of their birth. It is, perhaps, in the growing entertainments industry that a new type of self-made man has emerged to create positions whose role expectations can successfully be filled by those, particularly from the working class, who have a minimum of formal education.

CONCLUSION

In the modern version of controlled capitalism there is still a place for the entrepreneur, either working on his own or as a member of a team, who takes or creates opportunities. His behaviour is governed by the social structure and the norms of contemporary Britain. Change is expected of him as he plays his role, but sanctions work to constrain him from too great deviance or from particular forms of deviance. Thus, the social structure is an important determinant of whether entrepreneurs emerge or not, and of the direction in which economic change moves. The entrepreneurs who create new positions with new role expectations are those who make decisions that govern the new directions in which the economy will move. These men redraw the boundaries of tolerated behaviour. The analysis of the role of the entrepreneur is, therefore, important in relation to economic development and much of what has been said in this chapter may be seen as another dimension of the topic of social change, some aspects of which were considered in Chapter 3.

The role of the manager 6

The term manager covers all those who execute the details of policy made by entrepreneurs, whether individuals or in teams. The management of a concern is continuously present, whilst entrepreneurs may not always be there; boards of directors meet at intervals. Managers are of many kinds and hence have many roles. Two main divisions may be made. There are line managers, who supervise actual productive processes, and the staff, who bring special skills to their task of advising the line managers and of servicing the production side. Both categories may be entrepreneurs in the making. In a society where social mobility is relatively open and often nowadays achieved through success in the economy a manager may hope to be promoted so as to become a member of the entrepreneurial team. In many ways the contemporary equivalent of the selfmade man is the scholarship boy who reaches the board. Those in staff positions tend to be more specialised in their tasks and training; many are professionals, though there are also large numbers of technicians and clerks.

This is an élite group in the economy. Marx predicted a polarisation of the social classes, but it is this middle managerial group that has come to stand between the capitalist and the working classes. Furthermore, the managerial sector of the labour force is growing as a proportion of the whole. Between 1951 and 1961 the number of administrative, technical and clerical workers in British industry grew from 6,576,000 to 8,357,000. This represented a rise from 28·9 to 34·1 per cent of the total labour force. All except routine clerks receive incomes higher than most manual workers, but managers tend not to be large individual property owners in the way that capitalists and many members of entrepreneurial teams are. To the economy as a whole their skills and know-how represent a scarce form of capital that yields income. Hence some economists and writers on management have substituted 'organisation' as a factor of production in place of 'enterprise'. This is the group that Galbraith has called 'the technostructure'. He sees them as having more power than enterprise in the contemporary economic system. The view taken here, as the last chapter has indicated, is that enterprise can still be seen as a sociologically significant factor in the economy. Yet undoubtedly managers do have great power as a result of their resources of skill and know-how, and it is to a consideration of their position that we now must turn. We shall examine in succession the roles of the manager, the professional and the foreman.

THE MANAGER

His role

Simplification is necessary because of the many levels of manager. There are general managers, departmental and assistant managers, and so on down the hierarchy. Managers are also responsible for different types of concern—some industrial, others commercial. Yet there are some common elements in these different settings. They all have authority over the work of their subordinates and responsibility for seeing that it is carried out; they all make certain executive decisions and coordinate the activities of the organisations that they manage.

In this section consideration will be given mainly to line managers. The entrepreneur (or the entrepreneurial team in a joint stock company or even in a state-owned enterprise) decides the goals of the organisation at a general level and leaves to management the interpretation of these goals into detailed decisions. As one considers successively lower levels of management the decisions become increasingly routine; the range of expected behaviour grows narrower. The environment of managerial work would seem to be very similar in such large complex companies as I.C.I. and in the Civil Service. The manager in each of these bureaucracies has great security, regular salary rises, a pension, the chance of promotion up the hierarchy—often this is automatic up to a certain level. He has a good standard of life without wealth, a high income but little capital.

In this connection a recent American view of management is relevant. W. H. Whyte has coined the term 'organisation man'. His thesis is that a new type of manager has grown up within the large complex organisations, now more common in the contemporary economy. The beneficent organisation, whether private or state-owned, hires a young graduate, trains him, guarantees him slow promotion, and caters for his welfare. The hierarchy of management with its committee structure provides him with a secure series of roles to play. The manager is socialised into the culture of the organisation and this eases his geographical mobility as he is moved from one plant to another around the country, so that he can exist largely regardless of the local community, since he and his family are so securely rooted in the organisational community. Whyte believes that this is a true picture of many managers in big corporations in the U.S.A. Granick, who has investigated European (including British) managers, denies this to be the case in Europe. He found that managers were more individual, geographically less mobile and took more interest in the local community in which they lived when compared with those in the U.S.A.

The work in which managers are involved is largely the making of decisions, the nature of which varies with the setting. The personnel manager of a large factory is involved in decisions about hiring, firing and connected matters, whilst the assistant manager of a department is concerned with the way machinery is running and the delivery of raw materials. These problems are basically centred on the allocation of scarce resources to meet the goals of those at the top of the organisation. Many of the decisions to be made, particularly at the lower levels, will be routine; many can be made by rule of thumb. These latter, unlike those for which senior managers are responsible, do not allow varied solutions. Once the problem has been identified, the search for a solution begins and managers will try to take account of all the alternatives, in other words be as rational as possible. Yet very often it is impossible to know all the options that are open; for example, the reaction of workers to the offer of a new wage rate may not be predictable. Judgment must then be used and individuals with different backgrounds and training will view each problem from a different perspective. Hence there is room for a number of solutions. This is very true when managers are bargaining with other managers over such problems as production priorities. A very important time in any concern is when a new manager succeeds to his position. This event necessitates that all those with whom he interacts re-negotiate their expected patterns of behaviour. Indeed often the aim of the new appointment is to act as a catalyst for such a possibility of change.

Managers have obligations not only to other managers but also to workers. Labour relations are an important part of the work of most, especially line, managers. Decisions must be enforced. The manager has the problem of making his authority legitimate. Many base much of their authority on the qualities of their own personality, on what Weber called their charisma. This is particularly so in the case of top managers, but lower managers too can use the same basis for their authority. However, if they have excessive charisma, the lines of communication within the organisation may become fouled, since a low level manager who achieves great power will not wish to surrender information which may be the source of his power to those who are his superiors. The amount of charisma that is permissible at the lower levels varies according to the type of organisation concerned; reasearch workers may be allowed more than factory managers of a similar status, since the scientist is at the end of the chain of communication, whilst the manager is an important link.

One solution to the problem of ensuring managerial authority over workers that has gained a great following is that usually known as the human relations approach. This school was very popular in the interwar years and is still influential in both the U.S.A. and Britain. The fundamental belief here is that where authority has not been successfully achieved the problem lies in faulty relationships between workers and managers. This malfunction may be due to poor interpersonal relationships or to bad conditions of work; the correction of either, it is believed, will remove the source of irritation. The assumption, put simply, is that conflict between manager and workers is not a normal state, whilst agreement is.

More recently there has been a growing realisation that conflict is endemic to the interaction between manager and worker, since both tend to want more from the other than he is willing to give. The relationship is one of exchange; the manager gives a wage in return for labour whilst the worker gives his time and energy to earn money on which he may live. This is a stark picture. A full account would have to consider many other facets of the exchange. The worker, for instance, gains more satisfaction in some jobs than in others. He may bring to his role of worker a Marxist or a deferential ideology that is connected with the political role he plays off the job and this will influence the way in which he goes about any exchange with his manager. Managers also bring different resources to their attempt to enforce their power. The style of leadership which a manager adopts will have an effect on the bargain that he can make with his workers over his degree of power.

Managers all have to face this problem of establishing their authority. The strain involved in this position is met by adopting an ideology to explain their position. In this ideology managers will attempt to justify their degree of authority. Historical factors will be important in the way in which the managers in any one society develop their ideology. Few command and many obey, but the commands are given and obeyed in a different manner and spirit in Japan, Britain, the U.S.S.R. and Yugoslavia. In Japan many concerns are still run on the rather paternalistic lines commonly found during the early period of industrialisation which may be compared to the traditional master/servant relationship that still pertains in some rural areas in Britain. Power relationships in most British economic situations today may be termed constitutional, since much is determined by a process of collective bargaining that has continued over a number of years between management and unions, and much else is assumed as unwritten law by both parties. In the U.S.S.R. there is present, perhaps as a result of the Stalinist era, a more dictatorial element, particularly in comparison with Yugoslavia, where over the last fifteen years there has been an attempt to carry democracy onto the floor of the workshop.

The entrepreneur or the entrepreneurial team have most power since they take the ultimate risk in deciding general policy as a result of which the organisation in a capitalist system lives or dies. They alone know the crucial information upon which such decisions can be made. But there is no reason to assume that managers have no power. Some power adheres in their position as 'boss', but a very real source of power *vis-à-vis* higher managers is that they have scarce resources of information and know-how that those above them need and value. They can help or hinder the running of the concern by freely offering or withholding these resources. Furthermore, this power may be latent; it may not actually be applied very often, though naturally those over whom power is being wielded may test whether or not the power is real if they begin to doubt its existence. Thus, a manager can fire a worker for such misconduct as bad timekeeping, but he may not take this action, perhaps because labour is in short supply. Ultimately, however, the worker may become so lax that the manager uses his power because he feels that the behaviour may be imitated by other workers.

Change

A very important influence on the demands that are put upon management is the nature of the technology used. There is now a move away from the more specialised production of one-off units towards mass production. Even such large products as oil-tankers which were formerly made to the specifications of each individual customer are now sometimes built several to the same plan. The best example of this change is found in the rise of the mass production of clothes in place of the small tailor or dressmaker who made clothes to measure for his customers. Managers in technologies where unit production is still common, for instance, in the manufacture of heavy electrical equipment for hydroelectric plants, have far more complex decisions to make continuously. On the other hand, managers in the growing number of factories where the technology is based on mass production take fewer complicated and far reaching decisions, though the scope of such decisions when made is very great, but the day-to-day problems in these plants are of a much more routine nature.

The exact effect of this change on the type of manager needed is not yet known. But the more scientific and technical nature of the decisions to be made in plants of the newer type has increased the demand for managers with formal educational qualifications. The profile of the managerial sector of the labour force is changing so as to contain a greater proportion of highly educated managers. Partly because of this and partly due to the growing realisation of the key place that management must play in meeting Britain's recurring economic crises the status of the manager seems to have risen somewhat in comparison with the period before 1939.

The scale of units in British industry is growing and this, together with the increasing number of successful takeover bids, has brought about much managerial reorganisation. Those brought up to run small concerns have suddenly found themselves in large companies. Many problems have ensued. Nationalisation of industry provides examples of this happening. Thus, a number of relevant problems followed from the establishment of British Road Services. Many enterprises with very different modes of operation had to be moulded into one coordinated and cooperating whole with a hierarchy of management, each grade having a suitable salary and pension scheme. One of the problems following all such moves towards a rather mechanistic layout of the management structure is that ossification can ensue. Burns and Stalker have shown in their study of the growth of the Scottish electronics industry that a freer and more organic structure of management allows an organisation to adapt to change more easily.

Another group of problems is raised by the trend towards more rational methods of management and the need to introduce mechanisation into the office. This development affects all levels of management. Managers must learn new conceptual and logical skills to cope with the mass of information that is provided by, for instance, the adoption of computers. Mumford and Banks studied the way in which the introduction of computing into certain commercial and industrial concerns completely altered the processes by which decisions are made. For example, in banks the collection of information about the state of individual accounts passed from the higher managers to those lower in the chain of management. This changed, not just the type of skills needed at each level, but the distribution of power between levels. New grades were created with new powers, whilst the old grades had less. Often there is a delay before such effects make themselves fully apparent. Reactions to such changes vary according to the perceptions that members of the groups concerned have of the way in which they will be affected and this in turn varies greatly with the bargaining position, the level and the education of the managers concerned.

Recruitment and socialisation

Top managers are recruited from various sources. Some still come up the hard way, bred into the ways of their company, but many now have had a secondary education. In this connection Rosemary Stewart carried out a survey in the mid-1950s for the Acton Society Trust. She found that in fifty-one of the sixty-five privately owned British companies then having 10,000 or more employees 30 per cent of all managers had been to a grammar school and 20 per cent to a public school; more senior than junior managers had received a formal secondary education. More of the younger cohort of managers had been to such schools, but significantly, whereas a tenth of managers aged 55–59 had been to a public school, the proportion was a fifth for those aged 35–39. It would seem that the channels of mobility into lower management from state secondary schools may have become more open since the passing of the 1944 Education Act, but that this may not be the case for the senior posts.

Between a quarter and a third of top managers were graduates, though this proportion was greater among the younger men. A quarter of the top managers with degrees were Arts graduates from Oxford or Cambridge and this would seem a sign that the British tradition of amateur managers is still strong. Eighteen per cent of managers had professional qualifications, of whom half were engineers; many of the rest were chartered accountants and company secretaries. Amongst senior managers more had qualifications of the latter type, namely of a financial nature, than were technically qualified. Financial, rather than technical, skills seem to be valued more highly in top management.

Despite problems associated with the raising of capital and death duties family firms continue to exist and in such concerns managers are still recruited from the family. As Granick has indicated, this policy raises real problems for the recruitment of able middle managers, since the promotion of 'crown princes' puts a ceiling on the ambitions of men who are not members of the family. Similar problems are found in large companies that recruit senior managers from outside rather than by promotion, a policy often pursued to bring about the change that those managers already within the company do not want.

There is today a very strong connection between the level of the formal educational qualifications that a man possesses and the level of the labour force to which he is initially recruited, though success thereafter depends largely upon the effort and personality of the individual. To some extent socialisation within the company can be substituted for formal education and formerly the majority of managers learnt their jobs in this way, the managerial equivalent of the apprentice's 'sitting by Nellie'. Because of the way in which allocation to various types of secondary education is now organised a large proportion of really intelligent children today go to a university. In 1912 some 20 per cent of eighteen-year-olds with an I.Q. of over 120 were in universities; today the proportion is over 60 per cent. Despite the spread in the I.Q. scores of those in managerial posts managers do need high intelligence. Therefore, industrial concerns must go to the universities to recruit their young potential top managers. The tendency in many large companies is to recruit young graduates and to sponsor them into the company as future managers through trainee programmes in which they quickly 'go through the mill' to gain experience. Practical experience looms large in the ideology of British management and is also held in high regard by workers, who tend to rank expertise as important and to distrust what management sees as qualities of leadership, viewing these as mere 'cheek'.

THE PROFESSIONAL

His role

The classic professions are best exemplified by the doctor and lawyer. The peculiar mark of such occupations is that they are characterised by social interaction between a knowledgeable expert and an ignorant layman who seeks the benefit of their expertise. This relationship is at the roots of the institutions that surround a profession. Thus, a code of ethics is created to guard the powerless layman from the practitioner who has power to exploit his ignorance; control of entry to the ranks of the profession and surveillance of practitioners are ensured by the law, so that the standard of those practising can be guaranteed; formal qualifications from recognised educational institutions are demanded of intending members of the profession. These three points are illustrated in the case of the doctors by the Hippocratic oath, the General Medical Council and the degrees of the university medical schools.

During this century the number of groups aspiring to professional status has increased. Some, for example, teachers, may perhaps be called professionals. The characteristic relationships in the work situation are somewhat akin to those of the full professional and, as a result, the institutions surrounding the occupation have come to be very like those of the medical and legal professions. Others, for instance advertising men, cannot be considered sociologically as professionals, because the goal of their work is exploitative. In between these two examples lie many occupations—estate management and chartered surveying amongst others—that have some of the marks of a profession, but not all and, hence, may be termed near professions.

Professionals occupy a key position in the tertiary sector of the labour force and today large numbers work in staff positions in industry. Many are still self-employed and often have a very definite vocation to do their work. Their role is very diffuse and permeates their whole family life. The doctor's surgery is often in his house; the teacher may correct his pupils' exercises at home. But professionals who are employed as such in commercial or industrial concerns have a much more specific role, often of an advisory rather than a practising nature.

Changes

Professionals and members of near-professions who are employed in private or state-owned organisations are much more in the power of the non-professionals who often are line managers or entrepreneurs in such organisations. Because of the status of the professions in the past and the aura that still surrounds professional associations they are still considered as professionals even though they are now employees. Many of the newer professions have created associations, partly to try to establish their status and partly to bring countervailing power against those with whom they must deal, often from a position of weakness. The lawyer who is employed to give advice to a company is in a very different position to the practitioner who is self-employed or in a law partnership.

Serving these professionals and the other middle managers is a large force of technicians. Draughtsmen and laboratory staff may be cited as examples. These workers, like the growing element of clerical workers, are difficult to locate in the labour force as discrete categories. Thus, bank clerks are thought of as minor professionals, whilst many clerks have routine jobs that are akin to manual work in status and wage. But the majority, even of the routine clerical workers, tend to identify themselves with management, since their work situation is such that they constantly come into touch with managers. The status of clerical work was relatively high until this century, but the rise in the supply of educated workers and the increasing competition from women has altered the market situation so that the pay is not nearly so attractive to men. In addition, the work situation has been changed by the mechanisation of offices. The nineteenth-century counting house staffed by respectable men clerks has become a centre for processing documents manned by a few girls with a minimum of education.

It has been said that there has been a great growth in unionism amongst white collar workers, because they have seen that their interests often conflict with those of their employer despite their closeness to, and indeed in some cases identity with, management. If we first consider non-professionals, Bain has shown that the degree of unionisation is lower amongst white collar workers than amongst manual workers. In 1948, 53·1 per cent of manual and 28·8 per cent of white collar workers were in unions. By 1964 despite the great relative and absolute rise in tertiary employment these proportions were more or less unchanged, being respectively 51 per cent and 29·0 per cent. Membership is concentrated in the public service and is, therefore, heaviest in the civil service, local government and nationalised industries.

The higher status clerks tend to be members of associations that model themselves more on those representing professions. Collective bargaining is of little importance and some associations such as those for bank clerks, run professsional examinations. At this point the question may be raised: Is management itself a profession? There now exists the British Institute of Management and there is a growing number of examinations in management. Yet there is no control of entry to management, nor is there an ethical code. The associations of managers tend either to be pressure groups or educational bodies. Contemporary managers in industry or commerce may require formal education to do their jobs, but their work is still not characterised by that social relationship which is the peculiar mark of the classic, or even the near-profession.

Recruitment and socialisation

Not only is formal education vital for entry to the professions and to many white collar positions, but an early decision is needed so that the right curriculum may be pursued to meet the requirements of the chosen occupation. Such careers are unlike many jobs in that there is a regular pattern of steps of training and, in the early stages, of expected promotions. Chances of promotion vary with the sector in which the professional is employed. Careers in line management have more openings for promotion than do those in such staff positions as research and development.

The source of recruitment to any group is a major influence on the behaviour of those within the group. This is particularly noticeable in new occupations whose sources of recruitment do not yet follow an agreed pattern. Thus, Banks and others have shown how drug house representatives, though aspiring to professional status, have no agreed group norms about their behaviour towards their clients, namely doctors. So those who were formerly pharmacists with the formal qualification of M.P.S. adopted a professional stance, not pushing their products, whilst those who had originally been salesmen continued to behave towards the doctors as they had towards their former customers.

Even before entry to the labour force professionals start to learn the norms of behaviour expected of them in the roles that they will play. The future professional economist sees himself carrying out market research for a major retailing concern. After starting work professional socialisation continues. Box and Cotgrove have investigated the way in which scientists while they are still in training at the university build up expectations of the type of work that they will do as qualified chemists. If their initial post does not meet their anticipated expectations, they either change their views to meet the needs of that position, or leave it to take another which they hope will be more congenial, or, perhaps, stay where they are in a state of strain. Such movement from one professional position to another is in some ways easier for a professional than a non-professional manager, since the former is strongly oriented towards his professional community rather than towards his present employer. He is first a chemist and second works for 'X' company.

THE FOREMAN

The position of foreman generates much strain in those who fill it. Foreman are often considered by those under them as representatives of management, but may feel themselves to be one of the workers from whence they were recruited. To management the foreman may be seen as the man in the middle, neither a full member of the managerial team nor really a worker. In these circumstances foremen have difficulty in knowing to whom to relate. The classic description of the foreman as a 'marginal man' sees him trying to relate to both workers and managers, but failing to be accepted by either. He may, however, try to be 'one of the boys' in which case his style of authority and his resources of power will be very different from if he relates to management. In the latter case he will be more distant from those whom he supervises and more prone to come into conflict with them, whereas in the first case he will, at least in the eyes of management, be less capable of ensuring that his power is felt.

Because of these problems there is sometimes difficulty in recruiting foremen. In Britain, though not in the U.S.A., this is a terminal position, beyond which promotion is rare. In the past there was a supply of able men whose parents had not been able to afford prolonged schooling for them in their youth and these men provided a reservoir of potential foremen. Today this is no longer the case, since most children of ability now stay well beyond the minimum age for leaving school and, hence, in the future the position of foreman could well be filled by men of lesser ability. Foremen have to supervise processes of various types. At a very detailed level they do much the same work as line managers, namely planning and checking production, dealing with contingencies and reporting back to their immediate superior. Thurley and Hamblin noted that in four factories of very different types communicating was the main activity of foremen; they acted as a link in the channel of orders downwards and reports upwards that is vital to the control of production.

Social and economic changes since 1939 have made the position of foreman even more difficult to hold than it always has been. Many foremen have always been recruited from amongst craft workers because the skills that they possessed were important for the post. But technical changes have increased the amount of supervision done by specialised inspectors and much decision making of a craft nature is now done off the shop-floor in drawing or design offices. Differentiation amongst management has resulted in the creation of staff posts so that work that was formerly in the hands of a number of foremen is now carried out centrally. Labour officers, personnel managers and training officers today hire and fire, watch over problems of wages and supervise apprentices, all originally duties of foremen. These tasks provided foremen with much of their power, as they could find in them sanctions; for example, they might threaten to sack a man, they had control over bonus payments, and could also withhold from apprentices interesting chances to learn. Change has also come from the side of labour. Since 1939 the increasing strength of the unions in many industries, especially in engineering, led to the fixing of detailed piece rates through collective bargaining rather than by individual foremen. This trend has also worked to the lessening of the power of foremen over workers. The position of the foreman is in many ways always problematic and under contemporary conditions his role is increasingly equivocal.

CONCLUSION

The management of a modern large-scale enterprise is more complex than that of either a nineteenth-century large-scale concern or of a company run by a single entrepreneur. Any organisation may be seen as an uneasy coalition of entrepreneur or entrepreneurial team, managers, professionals, other white-collar workers, and workers. A constant process of bargaining goes on between all those within an organisation in order to decide whether the goals of those at the top will be allowed as the ends of the other members of the organisation or not, and to allocate the various resources that are available to meet whatever ends are decided upon allowing for all the constraints. The way in which managers at all levels legitimate their authority is crucial in these processes. Precedents may be followed or challenged; innovations may come either because of pressures from within the firm or as a result of pressures from outside. The management of any economic organisation, whether in the private or the public sector, is a changing and vital process.

The role of the worker 7

HIS ROLE

Constraints on the worker

One of the main trends in industrial organisation over the last century has been the growth in the proportion of the labour force who work under conditions of mass production. This trend has affected the behaviour expected of the worker in his job. On production lines workers are often restricted in their movements. The pace and the nature of their task will usually be determined for them by a manager in an office that may seem distant. The initiative that a skilled craftsman can display in his work is not demanded in such a position and the prior qualifications needed are few. To learn the behaviour demanded in any such position takes little time and, in view of the increased rate of technological change, this characteristic of many of the new jobs becoming available probably increases the adaptability of the labour force, as workers can leave declining industries or obsolescent processes and quickly learn what must be done in the newly created positions in the economy.

In the past unemployment was primarily due to the ups and downs of the trade cycle. In the interwar years the percentage of the labour force unemployed was at best under ten and at worst about twenty. However, since 1945 the rate of unemployment has never risen above 3 per cent. Yet the experience of past slumps has burnt deeply into the minds of the working class and even under conditions of full employment is expressed in antipathy to technical change which today is the main source of unemployment. There is a feeling that the occupancy of a particular position in the economy is the appropriated right of a worker, but as techniques change so do the positions available to workers and the behaviour expected in them. There is a need for more administrative and fewer unskilled workers, for more workers in the light engineering and fewer in the cotton textile industry.

As the quantity and the quality of the labour force alter, there is a continual process of bargaining between unions on behalf of workers and management over the agreed rules, whether formal or informal, that govern behaviour in the workplace; over, for example, pay and conditions, hours of work and who shall do what job. As relationships in the factory change 'the web of rule' governing work must alter. Conflict in results, some of which is organised and manifests itself in such group phenomena as strikes or lockouts, whilst some is unorganised, taking the form of increased labour turnover, higher rates of absenteeism, or poor time-keeping, behaviour that often seems to management to be simple 'bloody mindedness'.

Contemporary reactions

In their recent work on the contemporary situation of the worker Goldthorpe and Lockwood have posited three reactions to the social constraints imposed by capitalism in its present form. Firstly, some workers may still be described as 'traditional deferential workers'. This reaction occurs most frequently where the worker is in close continuous contact with his employer or with the middle class and, hence, is found especially in small businesses, small towns or rural areas, and in such positions as domestic work that are characterised by personal service. Under these conditions, traditionally associated with the early stages of industrialisation, workers accept their position and status without question, and value such non-economic rewards as friendliness with their employer, deferring easily to his opinions and accepting his values.

Secondly, we may speak of the 'traditional proletarian worker'. This response to work is usually connected with the old staple industries that formed the backbone of the British economy in the nineteenth century. These workers were separated physically from the middle class and from much of the rest of the working class. They evolved new norms in reaction to this isolation, tending to stress the need to cooperate in groups in order to build up countervailing power against the strength of the capitalists. They saw their immediate position in terms of 'us' and 'them'. This reaction is found in the old power centres of the economy, in the mines or on the railways, again as in the case of the deferential worker in declining sectors coping with the difficult consequences of technical change.

Lastly, there is the 'privatised worker'. This term has been used to describe those workers for whom work is not a central interest in their life, and who see their jobs merely as instrumental in earning money. This reaction is commonest in the large factories organised on mass production methods and typified by the car industry in which Goldthorpe and Lockwood carried out much of their research. This is an expanding part of the modern economy and the suggestion is that the privatised worker may be the worker of the future.

Some work done in the U.S.A. by Sayles and Kuhn is relevant at this point. They investigated another type of constraint, namely the way in which certain aspects of satisfaction with work were related to the technological conditions under which workers were employed. In a sample of 300 work groups they could discern four broad categories of worker. Those who were in groups where the technology demanded mainly unskilled labour were christened 'apathetic', in that they were least likely to engage in joint action in support of a grievance. Workers on assembly lines, for example, making cars, were called 'erratic', in that apparently trivial disputes with management flared up so that production was halted; one effect of this was to relieve the monotony of their jobs. A third group, the 'strategic' workers, were mainly skilled. Such craftsmen as maintenance electricians or welders were in key positions and could easily threaten the employment of many others both in their own factory and sometimes even in neighbouring sectors in the economy. Finally, there were what Sayles and Kuhn called 'conservative' workers. These men were keen to conserve their own control of the monopoly of skill and knowledge against any change. An example would be skilled men in printing. In this type of occupation strict rules about apprenticeship and demarcation, or who should do what jobs, are common.

Much work has been done, particularly in the U.S.A., on the way in which the privatised worker, who may also be categorised as apathetic or erratic, becomes alienated from his work. Blauner has shown how this feeling of alienation is made up of several separable strands. One important component is the degree of power a worker feels he has. Thus in a study of a large Lancashire bakery Daniel found that the vanmen, who were in many ways independent, having great control over their routes, hours and the way in which they dealt with the retailers that they visited, were much more satisfied with their jobs than were the bakers on the ovens. The latter worked specified but awkward hours, and had far less control over their methods of work. Again, a craftsman—a skilled mechanic or a carpenter—has more power over how he does his work than does a worker on most types of machine, who in his turn has more power than does a man at work on a production line. For the latter a second dimension of alienation is important; his task appears meaningless. Typically he is involved in a minute part of the production of a standardised product, unlike a craftsman, whose job is often concerned with the complete production of a unique article. Workers who carry out repetitive tasks have great difficulty in seeing that their present task has an important bearing on the quality of the final product. A third strand of alienation can be noticed at this point, that of involvement; alienated workers tend to be less involved in their jobs.

Finally, there is the element of alienation that is especially associated with Marx. The pre-industrial craftsman was so proud of his work that he was keen to be known as a tailor or a carpenter in the roles that he played away from his work; his work role pervaded his whole life and being. The man on the production line takes little pride in his task of tightening the nuts on offside front wheels and in his private life he is estranged from his economic self. He comes to find his real satisfaction elsewhere. Often his view is that he is showing to the world his real self in the role of husband or father that he plays at home in his family.

The car workers that Goldthorpe, Lockwood and others investigated at Luton fit well these dimensions of alienation. They felt powerless, their work was meaningless, and they were not really involved in it, their estrangement led to their concentration on their non-economic role in their families. Yet despite long hours and much overtime they were willing to exchange an unsatisfactory situation at work for the compensation of high pay secured by their strong situation in the labour market at a time of full employment. Their high pay was instrumental in their achieving high status, since it allowed them to buy the consumer goods that gave status in contemporary society.

Women workers

Much has been written in recent years about the changing role of women. A woman today, it is claimed, has two major roles to play, one at home and a new one at work. This argument overlooks the working role of women in the industrial revolution and the intermingling of economic and family work found under pre-industrial conditions in Britain and in most underdeveloped countries to this day. There are, however, some major changes in the economic role of women in contemporary Britain. Firstly, middle-class women now enter employment almost automatically, which was not the case a century ago. Secondly, women now continue to work after marriage and motherhood, and this is becoming true of the middle class as well as the working class. In 1963, 71 per cent of the women in the working population were aged twenty-five or over, 53 per cent were married, and of those who were married 90 per cent were twenty-five or over.

Not only is the age structure of women in the labour force changing, but they are now doing a very different type of job from those that they did in the nineteenth century. Then women were usually found in the textile industries or in domestic service. In June 1968 there were about 8·75 million women in the labour force, about three million of whom were still in industry, though they are not now so heavily concentrated in one group of industries, but work in many and particularly in such industries as light engineering where production line techniques are in use. But the major concentrations of employment for women are in distribution (1·6 m as against 1·3 m men), the professions (1·8 m against 0·9 m) and service industries (1·2 m against 1·0 m). Shops and offices are the main situations in which women work today. The white blouse has replaced the white cap.

This change reflects the increase in the tertiary sector of the labour force that is largely due to the stress on more rational modes of production. Certain problems are implicit in these changes. Only 5 per cent of the managers in manufacturing industry are women. Many women work at dull, routine tasks with a low chance of promotion in order to contribute what is usually the second pay packet in their families. A government survey published in 1968 showed that, though women named the desire for money as the first reason for their going out to work, the majority also put as a close second the desire for pleasant companions. Women are not so strongly oriented towards their work as are men. Not surprisingly on average they earn less than men and this is true even where they are doing the same work as men. This trend is most easily seen among the 10 per cent of women who work as members of professions (e.g., the health service) or in non-manual public service (e.g., teaching) where equal pay is given for equal work. The forces working to prevent women from becoming entrepreneurs also affect the careers of professional women, since many must break their careers with a period when they look after their babies. They thereby miss chances of promotion and even lose some of their skill or fail to keep up-to-date with developments in their profession. Men doing the same job are therefore more often able to fill the posts of responsibility that carry the higher rewards. In this way even where equal rates of pay have been gained the average earnings of women tend to be lower than those of men.

TECHNOLOGICAL CHANGE

Throughout the nineteenth century and up to about 1939 there seemed to be a move away from a heavy reliance by industry on craftsmen towards the employment of large numbers of semi-skilled and unskilled workers in factories either on machines or on production lines. Now the next major change appears to be an increased use of automation to control processes in factories. The exact repercussions on the demands for manpower are as yet not fully understood. It would appear that different skills are needed and that, though some routine work remains, much of the work, especially for men as opposed to women workers, may be of a more satisfying nature. In place of 'able workmen' the need seems to be for 'reliable workmen', since the degree of responsibility carried by those operating plants of this nature is very high. Small teams of men with a relatively high level of education or prior training run heavily capitalised plants, often working through the night without managerial supervision. The actual work done under such conditions is very similar to many white collar jobs, since it is clean, often involves book-keeping and forces regular contact with managerial staff. The increase in the proportion of such workers could somewhat offset the trend towards the rising numbers of privatised workers, since the constraints on the worker in a plant controlled by automation are more akin to those which a traditional deferential worker knew than those under which a privatised worker earns his living. Mumford and Banks have shown that the installation of computers in offices has a similar effect in that new and satisfying positions are created for some workers. However, the power situation is changed; some managers in banks have less control over accounts as much of their former work is now done at head office by the computer or by those who programme it. For others work becomes less personal and hence less satisfying; bank clerks punch tapes instead of entering up ledgers bearing the names of those to whom the accounts refer.

Technical change alters the positions available in the economy and the behaviour in those positions, that is, the role structure of the economy. Research has shown that difficulties ensue if both the formal and informal structures of the work situation do not match the new technology. Trist and Bamforth have shown how the post-war coal industry was hampered in its adoption of the longwall method of getting coal because the social organisation in the mines did not match the new technological organisation. This study showed how under the longwall system there were three shifts doing different tasks that depended upon each other for the success of the whole operation. Though these workers were interdependent, they never saw each other, so that each group tended to blame the others for anything that went wrong. Again, relationships with those in authority were poor because they were based on a structure devised to organise a different technique that relied on small individualistic teams rather than the new large specialised production groups.

Shift work, which has been normal in coal mining for many years, is now becoming more common, particularly in those sectors of the economy characterised either by heavy capital investment which must be worked around the clock to pay off high capital charges or by technical processes such as found in oil refineries or many chemical plants where damage would be done to plant by stopping production. These technical conditions are growing more common and between 1954 and 1964 the proportion of workers in manufacturing industry on shift work rose from 12 to 20 per cent. This has meant an increase in those for whom there is a problem of adjusting their economic role to the version of their family role still considered normal in our society. Fathers may want to sleep when children are ready to play or to make use of facilities that are only available to suit those who work from 8.0 a.m. till 5.0 p.m.

There are other aspects of technological change that affect the non-economic roles of workers. Thus greater capital intensity can lead to unemployment and some technical change can displace whole industries as seems to be happening in the case of the coal and the cotton industries and on the railways. Great social problems follow, especially in one-industry towns. Often, as Cottrell has shown, it is the most 'moral' by the norms of the community that suffer most. The worker who saves and buys his house loses much since the price of houses drops heavily; the man who built a small business loses all, as he cannot offset his losses against gains elsewhere in the way that a chain of shops can; the citizen who helped to run the church or the council or a club loses much satisfying social intercourse that is of benefit in helping to integrate the whole community. On the other hand the fly-by-night worker who wants the maximum wage can pull out of town without losing much, since he has not committed his all to the local community. It is worth noting that, from the point of view of social philosophy, the latter is following capitalist norms to the full, whilst the 'moral' worker gets the sympathy in our controlled version of the capitalist system.

COMPLIANCE

Power

Particularly in the sectors of the economy where workers are alienated from their jobs a major problem for those in power is to ensure that those in the organisation comply with the goals of the entrepreneurs or the entrepreneurial team. In some societies the solution was, indeed still is, that of physical coercion; this is the solution in slave economies, but it is not feasible in free societies. Although, as will be seen, different working conditions allow the application of different modes of control, the primacy of pay is indicated by the ideology of capitalism. A number of surveys, including that into the motives of women workers to which reference has just been made, have shown that money is the main reward for which workers do their jobs. For this sector of the labour force what Etzioni has called 'utilitarian' sanctions will be the most effective. Thus, entrepreneurs fix rates of pay and manipulate piece rates with the aim of encouraging workers in many jobs to give in exchange the maximum amount of labour.

Some white collar workers are in the same position, but conditions of status are major rewards for many; the location of their office, its decor and the numbers of those with whom they work are as important as their wage. The manipulation by management of the distribution of esteem can lead to workers sharing the same attitudes and values as entrepreneurs. White-collar workers especially may come to see capitalists or managers as significant others and to take entrepreneurial norms as their own. Such 'normative' control is very important in the case of such professionals among managers as research workers or lawyers, though in the case of many line managers, especially those on production or in sales, commission schemes provide powerful sanctions. Remuneration acts as a utilitarian control.

Where a worker has a true vocation for his job, as is the case with the clergy, a small reward is all that is needed to keep the man in his position since the work itself is his reward. In these cases all share the norms that ensure compliance. To some extent most professionals must have some feeling of vocation; doctors on night calls or lawyers working late at home expect no overtime pay. An important sociological principle that is applicable to all economic compliance can be seen at work in these cases. Control of recruitment enables the selection to any economic position only of those who already believe in the relevant norms or who are not likely to oppose the norms that they will meet when doing their new jobs. Furthermore, arrangements can be made to teach the necessary norms to those who come to the job concerned, whether specially selected or not. In other words careful recruitment and socialisation of workers can be substituted for utilitarian means to compliance, though when labour is in short supply as at times of full employment careful selection of workers, and even of some managers or professionals, is almost impossible.

Informal groups

Compliance is also difficult to achieve because of the way in which many economic groups come to form informal groupings within the structure of the organisation of their place of work. Very often these groups build up norms that are in opposition to those of the entrepreneur for whom they are working. In this way, printers, miners and jazz musicians have all been shown to have distinct occupational communities with their own customs and even languages. These occupations tend to be isolated either physically or by hours of work from other economic groups. Their work can easily spread over into non-work time; shop talk becomes common in the clubs and pubs frequented by miners. Whether considering professionals or blue-collar workers the presence of occupational communities has to be reckoned with in the power situation in any organisation since such groups give solidarity to employees. Also informal norms of output grow up. The famous studies under Mayo at the Hawthorne Works in the U.S.A. showed that even during a period of heavy unemployment, the 1930s, workers on piece rates were able to maintain their unofficial norms of output below what men could in fact produce on that machinery. Physical and social sanctions were used informally against those who offended.

In these cases the exchange process whereby the conflicting interests of labour and enterprise reach a truce situation that specifies pay and conditions of work becomes more difficult. The economic constraints under which different industries operate influence the development of such norms. Recently Lupton and Cunnison found in the Manchester area that informal norms developed in the engineering, but not in the garment, industry. In the latter case collective control of output was very hard to achieve. This industry is very competitive with many small firms so that once a job is lost work of the same nature is not readily found elsewhere. In addition, because the capital costs of establishing a new firm are small, new units can be set up relatively easily. Thus garment workers tend to look after their own interests rather than those of some informal group. In the engineering industry units are large and competition less intense. Under these economic conditions the social response of the workers is to cooperate in informal groupings in order to guard each other's interests by setting up unofficial norms about how much is to be produced and how to calculate piece rates in their own interest rather than in those of the management. Economic power, like political power, is constrained by the compliance of those who are to obey.

TRADE UNIONS

Theory

The whole problem of power in industry and the achievement of compliance through setting specific wage rates leads to some consideration of trade unions. Fox has recently defined trade unions as 'representative institutions which participate with management in a process of joint decision making on issues of day-to-day management'. Exchanges constantly go on between the representatives of labour and capital. These are governed by the ideologies held by each economic group and take place within the institutions that have grown up for this purpose, namely employers' associations, unions and certain organisations supplied by the state. As indicated in Chapter 2, since the 1890s the state has provided certain facilities to assist the process of bargaining on one condition, namely that it should only be called on to help by providing arbitrators, conciliators or mediators if necessary. The state does not intervene unless requested except in one case; under the system of the Wages Council the state will establish statutory machinery for fixing wages if the workers in an occupation are too weak to provide this for themselves.

Normally bargaining is between unions and employers or their associations. The ideology that governs employers may be described in a rather oversimplified way in two sentences. Management is the only source of authority in any industrial organisation, and, therefore, to most managers Fox's definition of a trade union, stressing as it does 'joint' decisions, would be unacceptable. Secondly, leadership is vital for unity, so that conflict is not the normal state in industry but is the result of poor management. Men holding such beliefs inevitably come into opposition with those representing labour whose ideology rests on the assumption that by using their power to withdraw their labour they can increase the share of the national income going to labour. Just as the ideology of management is based on a view that industrial sociologists have shown to be in large part misconceived, since conflict is endemic to any industrial, or other, organisation, so too is there some doubt whether in fact the unions are basing their conduct on sound reasoning. Kerr has shown that the share of the national income received by labour in Britain since 1870 has risen from just under 40 per cent to just over 40, but there is no certainty that this can be attributed to the activities of the unions. Certainly any rise in the proportion during the second world war was mainly due to the rise in the proportion of the labour force in such highly paid employment as engineering.

However, such rational considerations do not govern the contemporary process of industrial bargaining, which is what must be explained. The exchanges that take place within this context govern most of the conditions of work in industry. The process is complicated by the continual changes in the relevant technologies and in the competitive situation of particular industries. At any time in any job there is a web of rules, explicit and implicit, that governs the expected behaviour in any industrial position. As with any role there are what Gouldner has called 'patterns of indulgency', or ranges of tolerated behaviour, which are informally permitted though outside the present official rules. Very often merely to tighten up on the informal rules, perhaps by demanding more rigid time-keeping, can precipitate an unofficial strike. All industrial agreements are temporary, since redefinition of roles must be made frequently to meet economic change. Thus a new process that affects two skilled crafts can easily lead to a demarcation dispute to settle which occupation does some part of the task.

This process of definition and redefinition is carried out through collective bargaining between employers, or their representatives, and the representatives of labour. Though this is true in the case of blue-collar and some clerical workers, individual bargaining is more common in the case of white-collar workers with higher status, and managers. The power of those who participate in all these negotiations depends on the resources available to them in their economic situation. Thus, if the demand for their product is high, workers are in a strong position since the withdrawal of their labour would jeopardise the profits of the company; alternatively, a low level of demand enables the entrepreneur to do without workers with less fear of missing the chance to earn profits. Again, if the supply of labour to the industry or to some particular position, perhaps a craft, is tight, the union is in a stronger position than if labour is abundant.

There is something of a paradox involved in this situation, since workers basically have a dual allegiance to both their union and the firm for which they work. Dean quotes a worker in a meat packing plant in Chicago who showed this clearly. 'The company gives me my job and I am grateful. The union protects my dignity as an individual, and that is essential too.' The conflict is there, but so too is the need to work as a team with management. The constant dialogue between labour, capital and enterprise is at present in Britain carried on through collective bargaining leading to truce situations, creating new rules. These agreements can only be temporary, as changes in the economy will soon alter the assumptions upon which they are founded. Conflict and consensus alternate.

The unions today

Much collective bargaining is done today at the level of the industry and hence on a national basis. Management sees this as a chance to divide one part of the managerial role into two segments. The first concerns its relations with unions, often with several in one plant, and this is isolated from the second segment which concerns its relations with the workers in a plant. By this strategy the entrepreneur or manager sees himself as still master in his own factory and hopes to conduct his relations with his workers in such a way that they identify with the firm. Various techniques of joint consultation within the plant have been evolved to consider specific problems of production and of working conditions, though often the effect has been that instead of identifying with the firm the workers have lost their faith in their own local leaders, who in the eyes of the workers have cooperated with the enemy, namely with capital.

As national bargaining has grown in importance unions have become bureaucracies with large permanent staffs who negotiate, keep records, manage union funds, do research and keep in touch with members. Great efforts are made to keep in touch with the rank and file and to preserve the norms traditional to unions by recruiting only former workers to line positions in union management. But the constraints that work towards conservatism in most bureaucracies and the problem of communicating with members have tended to cut off workers from their leaders. One result has been the revival since about 1940 of the shop steward movement, started originally in the First World War. This is especially strong in the engineering industry where conditions favour one man representing one workshop, because there is much local negotiation at the level of individual shops about rates of pay for specific unique products. The shop steward is in touch directly with the grievances of workers on the job and has in many places become the heir to the militant tradition of the unions.

From 1892 to 1964 the membership of the unions grew by 539 per cent from 1·5 to 10 million, but during this period the numbers in the labour force rose by only 67 per cent. Thus the density of unionism, that is, the actual membership expressed as a proportion of the potential membership, rose from 16 to 47 per cent. This last figure varies by occupational group, but is lower than might perhaps be expected due to low densities in two particular sectors. Firstly, women are underrepresented in unions; though they make up a third of the labour force, in 1965 only 21·7 per cent of women workers were members of unions. Secondly, as the work of Bain quoted in the last chapter has shown, the numbers of clerical workers has grown since 1945, but they still seem loath to become less deferential and join unions.

One result of the move to national bargaining seems to be that long strikes involving large numbers of workers have become less frequent but only at the expense of more short, small, often unofficial strikes. Despite the prevailing view that much time is lost through strikes Lerner (in Prest) has calculated that the average amount of time lost per head was 0·339 of a day in 1957, 0·213 in 1959 and 0·227 in 1962, whilst about 11·5 days per year are lost through illness or injury. Yet there are big differences in the incidence of strikes by industry. As Kerr and Siegal have shown this is an international phenomenon. Mining, maritime and dock workers had a high propensity to strike in all the eleven countries that they considered, whilst railway and agricultural workers all showed a low propensity. It would seem that those industries where workers form a relatively homogeneous and cohesive group, isolated either geographically or normatively from the rest of the community, provide conditions in which strikes are likely to occur. On the other hand, where workers are integrated as individuals into the community around them and are not able to co-operate with similar workers, strikes are much rarer. Once again the industrial structure is a major constraint on the behaviour of those working within it.

RECRUITMENT

Occupational choice

The concept of a labour market assumes the free flow of labour to the highest reward. In reality a worker has little or no sensation of being in a labour market. A science graduate may have a reasonably accurate idea of what positions and salaries are open to him, but a worker is ignorant of the full range of jobs and wages open to him, even in his own locality. Various institutions exist to channel workers into jobs. There are advertisements, at national level mainly for managerial and professional jobs and at local level usually for vacancies at the lower levels of the labour force. Personnel departments exist in many companies to hire labour, even of managerial and professional status. Trade unions sometimes assist craftsmen to find new positions. The state provides a network of employment exchanges which are mostly used by the lower levels of the labour force, but which also maintain registers of professional vacancies. The Youth Employment Service fulfils a similar function for the school leaver. There are also private employment agencies, mainly for three types of labour, namely managers, teachers and domestic servants. In addition, workers often find jobs without the help of such institutions—often through friends or relatives. A survey by Scott and others found that in 1954 at one large iron and steel works in Cheshire between a quarter and a fifth of the workers had been 'spoken for' in this manner.

As already indicated the boundaries of the labour market vary by the grade of labour. The current phrase, 'the brain drain', which refers to the emigration of highly educated men, indicates the international nature of the market for many high grade jobs. For most managers and professionals the labour market is national, but for the rest of the labour force the boundary in Britain is effectively less than one day's journey from home, and in a survey carried out in 1945–49 about half of the working population had only worked in one town, whilst the rest had only worked in two on average.

To speak of 'choice' of occupation is perhaps stretching the common meaning of this noun, since the majority of workers seeking work are constrained by the positions available locally, which in a mining village, for instance, covers a very narrow range. Furthermore, possible first choices are restricted by the pathways through which the young reach the age at which they leave school. On the whole a working-class child tends to be fitted for a different range of jobs from a middle-class child, and an education at a grammar school leads to a different level of the labour force from that given in a secondary modern school or even in the early leaving streams of a comprehensive school.

Once the point of choice is reached an exchange process occurs in which the young person with more or less rationality balances the tangible and intangible satisfactions judged to flow from the various jobs on offer against the tangible and intangible costs involved in doing each job. There are great variations in the age at which the decision must be made and in its irrevocability. The extremes are exemplified, on the one hand, by the temporary choice of such unskilled seasonal labour as hop-picking which requires little training and is known to be a short-term job and, on the other hand, by a medical career, which necessitates a decision early in secondary school to do a course biased towards science subjects. This latter example also shows the increasing finality of many choices of managerial and professional careers, since the further the young person goes along the pathway towards his ultimate goal, the more irrevocable his choice becomes. At each stage he narrows his chance for manoeuvre. At fourteen he has the chance of becoming a doctor, dentist, or a pure or applied scientist. Ten years later his options have narrowed to becoming, perhaps, either an eye surgeon or an ear, nose and throat specialist.

The increase in the rate of technological change means that the positions that many originally choose and whose role they thoroughly learn may more frequently become redundant. Thus increasingly they must re-enter the labour market and go through the process of choosing a job again, still under the influence of local opportunities and of the pathway by which they reached their present situation, though now with some added experience. Also of relevance is the reason for leaving their last job. Those redundant because of technological change will probably have a better chance of a new job than those who were dismissed on disciplinary grounds.

Job or career?

Finally we must consider the life cycle of the worker within the economic structure. Few workers can hope for the orderly progression of positions in the same field that most professionals have been seen to expect and to call a career. Some occupations of low status do provide careers. In mining, men do proceed from the jobs of less to those of greater skill that are paid more and are nearer to the coal face and then with increasing age move back to less arduous work. Lorry drivers tend to start as short distance 'shunters', move to irregular long distance tramping, then on to long distance night trunking before, finally, with age they return to shunting. For perhaps the majority such careers are impossible, particularly today, as the rate of labour turnover due to technological change is such that few entering first jobs now can hope to be doing the same work when they retire.

Some workers leave jobs soon after starting them, usually within the first six months, because for personal or other reasons they are unable to learn to survive in that particular environment. Many stay and become long-service workers, possibly ultimately receiving promotion. In the mid-1950s Stewart found that in a number of the large companies she investigated the average service before promotion to chargehand was eight years and to foreman, sixteen years. To rise beyond this level is rare in Britain, as foreman is seen as a terminal position. Seniority is very important in promotion. Thus in the iron and steel industry progress up a furnace team to the position of first hand melter is entirely a matter of seniority and attempts to introduce promotion by merit have failed, largely because of opposition from unions.

In Stewart's sample 60 to 70 per cent of the workers interviewed said that they were 'very interested' in promotion, but only half these men had applied for promotion when vacancies were advertised. In fact, many workers recognised the unlikelihood of promotion and many had seriously considered starting a small business on their own account. From the evidence in their sample Goldthorpe and Lockwood and others conclude that 'starting up their own business was an idea with somewhat more appeal for affluent workers than that of gaining promotion'; white-collar workers were keener on promotion than going into business on their own account. Another investigation into attitudes towards promotion was carried out by Sykes in a Scottish iron and steel works and yielded somewhat similar results. Clerks were in favour of promotion, as it raised no problems to them in their way of life, but steel workers were against it, because they would lose their friends and they saw those who were promoted as traitors to their class, though in the Scottish tradition these workers were not against upward social mobility as such, merely against its direct manifestation amongst those close to them in their own plant.

CONCLUSION

These last findings exhibit two important strands in this book. First, the reactions of the clerks and steel workers to their social surroundings once again show the crucial importance of such constraints on the behaviour of men in their work. Second, both studies stress very clearly the way in which *laissez-faire* permeates the economic system. When workers are willing to become recruits to enterprise or clerks the servants of capital, this is indeed, like it or not on political grounds, a tribute to the strength of the contemporary version of the capitalist ideology.

References and further reading

General

Annual Abstract of Statistics, H.M.S.O.

Also see the most recent edition of

A. R. Prest, ed. *The U.K. Economy. A manual of applied economics*, Weidenfeld & Nicolson, 1966.

Chapter 1 : Economic ideas

W. J. Barker, *A History of Economic Thought*, Pelican, 1967.

C. S. Belshaw, *Traditional Exchange and Modern Markets*, Prentice-Hall, 1965.

T. B. Bottomore and M. Rubel, *Karl Marx : Selected Writings in Sociology and Social Philosophy*, Penguin (Pelican), 1961.

K. Davis, *Human Society*, Collier-Macmillan, 1948, chapter 7, 'Property'.

R. Firth, ed. *Themes in Economic Anthropology*, Tavistock Publications, 1967.

J. K. Galbraith, *The New Industrial State*, Hamish Hamilton, 1967.

R. L. Heilbroner, *The Making of Economic Society*, Prentice-Hall, 1962.

A. Marshall, *Principles of Economics*, 8th edition, Macmillan, 1920.

G. Myrdal, *Beyond the Welfare State*, Duckworth, 1960; Methuen Univ. Paperbacks, 1965.

J. Robinson, *Economic Philosophy*, Penguin, 1964.

J. S. Schumpeter, *Capitalism, Socialism and Democracy*, Allen & Unwin, 1943.

N. J. Smelser, *The Sociology of Economic Life*, Prentice-Hall, 1963.

M. Weber, *The Theory of Social and Economic Organisation*, ed. T. Parsons, W. Hodge, 1947.

Chapter 2 : British economic institutions

E. H. Phelps Brown, *The Economics of Labor*, Yale University Press, 1962.

J. H. Dunning and C. J. Thomas, *British Industry*, 1961, n.e. Hutchinson, University Library, 1966.

Florence, P. Sargant, *Ownership, Control and Success of Large Companies*, Sweet & Maxwell, 1961.
W. Friedman, 'Changes in property relations', *Transactions of Third World Congress of Sociology*, vol. 2, 1956.
G. Grossman, *Economic Systems*, Prentice-Hall, 1967.
C. W. Guillebaud, *Wage Determination and Wages Policy*, 2nd ed., Nisbet, 1967.
H. F. Lydall and D. G. Tipping, 'The distribution of personal wealth in Britain', *Oxford Bulletin of Statistics*, February 1961.
G. Routh, *Occupations and Pay in Great Britain*, Cambridge University Press, 1965.
R. M. Titmuss, *Income Distribution and Social Change*, Allen & Unwin, 1962.

Chapter 3: Economic change

O. Banks and W. H. Scott, *Men, Steel and Technical Change*, H.M.S.O./D.S.I.R., 1957.
Florence, P. Sargant, *The Logic of British and American Industry* (1953), 2nd edn, Routledge & Kegan Paul, 1961.
E. E. Hagen, *On the Theory of Social Change*, Tavistock Publications, 1964.
P. Halmos, ed. 'The development of industrial society', *Sociological Review Monograph No. 8*, Keele, 1964.
B. F. Hoselitz and W. E. Moore, *Industrialization and Society*, Unesco, 1963.
C. Kerr, J. T. Dunlop, F. H. Harbison and C. A. Myers, *Industrialism and Industrial Man*, Heinemann, 1962.
P. W. Musgrave, *Technical Change, the Labour Force, and Education*, Pergamon, 1967.
P. W. Musgrave, 'The educational profile of two British iron and steel companies with some comparisons national and international', *British Journal of Industrial Relations*, July 1966.
J. W. Woodward, *Management and Technology*, H.M.S.O./D.S.I.R., 1958.

Chapter 4: The role of the consumer

B. Abel-Smith and P. Townsend, *The Poor and The Poorest*, Bell, 1965.
M. Abrams, *The Teenage Consumer*, London Press Exchange, 1959.
H. Behrend, 'Price images, inflation, and national income', *Scottish Journal of Political Economy*, Edinburgh, November 1966.

T. Burns, 'The study of consumer behaviour: a sociological view', *European Journal of Sociology*, Paris, July–December 1966.
R. F. Hamilton, 'Affluence and the worker: the German case', *American Journal of Sociology*, September 1965.
G. Katona, *The Mass Consumption Society*, McGraw-Hill, 1964.
E. Katz and P. Lazarsfeld, *Personal Influence*, Chicago Free Press, 1955.
H. Liebenstein, 'Band-wagon, snob and Veblen effects in the theory of consumer demand', *Quarterly Journal of Economics*, Cambridge, Mass., May 1950.
H. F. Lydall, *British Incomes and Saving*, Oxford, Blackwell, 1955.
D. Riesman and H. Roseborough, 'Careers and consumer behaviour', in L. H. Clark, ed. *Consumer Behaviour*, New York University Press, 1955.
H. Roseborough, 'Some sociological determinants of consumer spending', *Canadian Journal of Political Science*, Toronto, August 1960.
G. P. Stone, 'City shoppers and urban identification: observations on the social psychology of city life', *American Journal of Sociology*, July 1954.

Chapter 5: The role of the entrepreneur

D. F. Aberle and K. D. Naegele, 'Middle-class father's occupational role and attitudes toward children', *American Journal of Orthopsychiatry*, April 1952.
The Acton Society Trust, see R. Stewart.
W. L. Baldwin, 'The motives of managers, environmental restraints and the theory of managerial enterprise', *Quarterly Journal of Economics*, May 1964.
F. Barth, ed. *The Role of the Entrepreneur in Social Change in Northern Norway*, Oslo 1963.
R. V. Clements, *Managers: A Study of their Careers in Industry*, Allen & Unwin, 1958.
A. H. Cole, *Business Enterprise in its Social Setting*, Harvard University Press, 1959.
C. Erickson, *British Industrialists: Steel and Hosiery. 1850–1950*, Cambridge University Press, 1959.
P. S. Florence, see p. 109.
W. E. Henry, 'The business executive: the psychodynamics of a social role', *American Journal of Sociology*, Chicago, November 1948.
K. Mayer, 'Business enterprise: traditional symbol of opportunities', *British Journal of Sociology*, June 1953.

D. C. McClelland, *The Achieving Society*, Princeton, N.J., 1961
D. R. Miller and G. E. Swanson, *The Changing American Parent*, Wiley, 1958.
W. Miller, ed. *Men in Business*, Harper & Row, 1952.
F. Redlich, 'Economic development, entrepreneurship and psychologism: a social scientist's critique of McClelland's Achieving Society', *Explorations in Entrepreneurial History*, Cambridge, Mass., Fall 1963.
E. Salin, 'Origins of business: European entrepreneurship', *Journal of Economic History*, New York, Fall 1962.
J. S. Schumpeter, see p. 108.
F. X. Sutton, S. E. Harris, C. Kayser and J. Tobin, *The American Business Creed*, Cambridge, Mass. Schocken; Bailey Bros., 1956.
R. Stewart, *Managers for Tomorrow*, H.M.S.O./D.S.I.R., 1957.
R. R. Wohl, 'The "Rags to Riches" story; an episode of secular idealism' in R. Bendix and S. M. Lipset, *Class*, *Status and Power*, 2nd edn, Routledge & Kegan Paul, 1967.

Chapter 6: The role of the manager

G. S. Bain, 'The growth of white collar unionism in Great Britain', *British Journal of Industrial Relations*, November 1966.
J. A. Banks, S. M. T. Kaxte, R. E. A. Mapes and C. W. M. Wilson, 'The drug house representative', *Sociological Review*, July 1964.
T. Burns, and G. M. Stalker, *The Management of Innovation*, Tavistock Publications, 1961; n.e. 1966.
R. Bendix, 'Industrialization, ideologies, and social structure', *American Sociological Review*, October 1959.
S. Box and S. Cotgrove, 'Scientific identity, occupational selection, and role structure', *British Journal of Sociology*, March 1966.
I. C. Cannon, 'Ideology and occupational community: a study of compositors', *Sociology*, May 1967.
R. M. Cyert, and J. G. March, 'A behavioral theory of organizational objectives' in M. Haire, ed. *Modern Organization Theory*, Wiley, 1959.
A. Etzioni, *A Comparative Analysis of Complex Organizations*, Collier-Macmillan, 1961.
B. B. Gardner and W. F. Whyte, 'The man in the middle: position and problems of the foreman', *Applied Anthropologist*, Boston, Mass., Spring 1945.
D. Granick, *The European Executive*, Doubleday; Weidenfeld & Nicolson, 1962.

F. Harbison and C. A. Myers, *Management in the Industrial World*, McGraw-Hill, 1959 (see chapter 16, W. H. Scott, 'Management in Great Britain').
H. Hartmann, 'Managers and entrepreneurship: a useful distinction', *Administrative Science Quarterly*, Ithaca, N.Y., March 1959.
E. Mumford and O. Banks, *The Computer and the Clerk*, Routledge & Kegan Paul, 1967.
K. Prandy, *Professional Employees*, Faber, 1965.
K. E. Thurby and A. C. Hamblin, *The Supervisor and his Job*, H.M.S.O./D.S.I.R., 1963.
W. H. Whyte, *The Organisation Man*, Penguin (Pelican), 1960.
J. W. Woodward, *Management and Technology*, H.M.S.O./D.S.I.R., 1958.

Chapter 7: The role of the worker

R. Blauner, *Alienation and Freedom*, University of Chicago Press, 1964.
W. F. Cottrell, 'Death by dieselization: a case study in the reaction to technological change', *American Sociological Review*, June 1951.
W. W. Daniel, 'A comparative consideration of two industrial work groups', *Sociological Review*, March 1963.
L. R. Dean, 'Union activity and dual loyalty', *Industrial and Labour Relations Review*, Ithaca, N.Y., July 1954.
N. Dennis, F. Henriques and C. Slaughter, *Coal is Our Life*, Eyre & Spottiswoode, 1956.
A. Fox, 'Managerial ideology and labour relations', *British Journal of Industrial Relations*, November 1966.
H. Gavron, *Woman's Two Roles*, Penguin (Pelican), 1966.
J. H. Goldthorpe and D. Lockwood, 'Affluence and the British class structure', *Sociological Review*, July 1963.
J. H. Goldthorpe, D. Lockwood, F. Bechhofer and J. Platt, *The Affluent Worker: Industrial Attitudes and Behaviour*, Cambridge, 1968.
A. W. Gouldner, *Wildcat Strike*, New York, Antioch Press, 1954.
P. G. Hollowell, *The Lorry Driver*, Routledge & Kegan Paul, 1968.
G. K. Ingham, 'Organisational size, orientation to work and industrial behaviour', *Sociology*, September 1967.
C. Kerr, 'Trade-unionism and distributive shares', *American Economic Review*, May 1954.
C. Kerr and A. Siegel, 'The interindustry propensity to strike: an international comparison', in A. Kornhauser, R. Dubin and A. Ross, *Industrial Conflict*, McGraw-Hill, 1954.

D. Lockwood, 'Some variations in working class images of society', *Sociological Review*, November 1966.

T. Lupton and S. Cunnison, 'Workshop Behaviour' in M. Gluckman, ed. *Closed Systems and Open Minds*, Oliver & Boyd, 1964.

E. Mumford and O. Banks, see p. 112.

P. W. Musgrave, 'Towards a sociological theory of occupational choice', *Sociological Review*, March 1967.

S. R. Parker, R. K. Brown, J. Child and M. A. Smith, *Sociology of Industry*, 1968.

R. and R. Rapoport, 'Work and family in contemporary society', *American Sociological Review*, June 1965.

L. Sayles, *Behavior of Industrial Work Groups*, Wiley, 1958.

W. H. Scott and others, *Technical Change and Industrial Relations*, Liverpool University Press, 1956.

N. Seear, *The Position of Women in Industry*, Royal Commission on Trade Unions and Employers' Associations, Research Paper No. 11, H.M.S.O., 1968.

R. Stewart, see p. 111.

A. J. M. Sykes, 'Some differences in the attitudes of clerks and of manual workers', *Sociological Review*, November 1965.

E. L. Trist and K. W. Bamforth, 'Some social and psychological consequences of the longwall method of coal-getting', *Human Relations*, February 1951.

H. Wilensky, 'Work, careers and social integration, *International Social Science Journal*, No. 4, Unesco, 1960.

Index